# THE IMPACT OF GOD

# The Impact of God

## Soundings from St John of the Cross

Iain Matthew

**Hodder & Stoughton**
LONDON SYDNEY AUCKLAND

Copyright © Iain Matthew 1995

First published in Great Britain in 1995

The right of Iain Matthew to be identified as the Author of
the Work has been asserted by him in accordance with the
Copyright, Designs and Patents Act 1988.

10  9

British Library Cataloguing in Publication Data
A record for this book is available from the British Library

ISBN 0 340 61257 6

Typeset by Hewer Text Composition Services, Edinburgh
Printed and bound in Great Britain by
Clays Ltd, St Ives plc

The paper and board used in this paperback are natural recyclable
products made from wood grown in sustainable forests.
The manufacturing processes conform to the environmental
regulations of the country of origin.

Hodder and Stoughton
A Division of Hodder Headline Ltd
338 Euston Road
London NW1 3BH
www.madaboutbooks.com

# Contents

To Elizabeth and Monk Matthew
with a son's love and thanks

# Acknowledgments

My thanks first to those who have come to talks or retreats on John, and for the comments they have made.

Sincere thanks to Rowan Williams, Norbert Cummins, María del Sagrario Rollán, Ross Collings, Dafyd Miles Board, and to members of the Centro Internacional, Avila, for insights which have formed part of this book. In particular I am indebted to the teaching and writing of Federico Ruiz, particularly his *Introducción a San Juan de la Cruz* (Madrid, BAC 1968) and *Místico y Maestro* (Madrid, EDE 1986), and to the teaching of Maximiliano Herraiz. These have been uniquely inspiring.

Sister Teresa Benedicta OCD has read the manuscript in various forms and has been just great! My heartfelt thanks to her.

I am very grateful to Jean Vanier for writing the Foreword.

I wish to convey my gratitude to Teresa de Bertodano for her editorial skill and for her encouragement; also to Carolyn Armitage, to Elspeth Taylor, and to Eric Major, all of Hodder and Stoughton, for their kind assistance. Thanks to Roseann and Sue Marindin, to Olivia Caddell and to Anne King for their helpful reflections.

To Frs Jerry Fitzpatrick, John Kelly, Ronan Murphy and John Butters, the community of El Desierto de Las Palmas, and my own community, my thanks for their support.

Scripture quotations, unless otherwise noted, are from the *Revised Standard Version* (CE, Oxford University Press 1966). Details in the map are drawn from *Dios Habla en la Noche*, various authors (Madrid, EDE 1990). Crisógono de Jesús, *Vida de San Juan de la Cruz*, eleventh edition Madrid, Biblioteca de Autores Cristianos 1982), has proved useful; so too notes in the *Obras Completas* mentioned below. There are excerpts from the English translation of the *Rite of Holy Week* (© 1972, International Committee on

English in the Liturgy, Inc, all rights reserved). Some ideas and expressions in the present book coincide with my article, 'John and daily life' in *A fresh approach to St John of the Cross* (Slough, St Paul's, formerly St Paul Publications, 1993).

The translations of the *Living Flame* and *Dark Night* poems, and of stanza 32 of the *Canticle*, are by Marjorie Flower OCD (*The poems of St John of the Cross*, published by the Carmelite nuns, Varroville, Australia). John's poetry is indeed untranslatable; but Sister Marjorie has so entered into the verses that her version conveys their warmth of feeling and lightness of touch in a quite beautiful way. It manages too to follow the metre and rhyme sequence of the original Spanish. Sincere thanks to her.

Translations of the prose and remaining poetry of St John of the Cross are my own. I have used the *Obras Completas*, edited by José Vicente Rodríguez, Federico Ruiz, fifth edition (Madrid, EDE, 1993). My aim has been to transmit the spirit and vivacity of the original. This has led to some modifications in favour of contemporary usage ('alma', 'soul', is sometimes translated 'person'). Since the Christian assumes the role of bride in John's writings, I generally refer to the Christian as 'she' (which also helps the clarity of the sentence). The translations by Kieran Kavanaugh, Otilio Rodriguez (Washington, Institute of Carmelite Studies 1991) and by E. Allison Peers (Tunbridge Wells, Burns and Oates 1935) remain important reference points.

# Foreword

This is a book for which – perhaps unconsciously – I have been waiting. Christians struggled for many years under the power of an Almighty God, fearful of this Law-giver and of the punishments they would receive if they did not obey him, and hopeful of the rewards if they did. Then the pendulum swung. Fear of authority was replaced by a negation of authority. Jesus became Emmanuel, God-with-us, the gentle and kind friend, who blesses everything and who makes few demands. It was a positive swing but something was lost in the transition: Jesus lost his divinity, his sacredness, the flame of love that purifies, hurts and burns in order to lead us into something totally new: the ecstasy of love and a peace that surpasses all human understanding.

It is important to come back to the true face of God, the God of love, a love that burns and purifies and leads to the Wedding Feast; that *is* the Wedding Feast. Today we have a particular need of John: John of the Cross, John of Pain, to help us discover this God of Love. Iain Matthew helps us to discover the true John.

This book reveals a humble, little John (he was even physically small), a John who suffered pain and poverty, a John of humble origins. It shows us how John met and loved Teresa of Avila and how this beautiful woman brought him hope, encouragement, inspiration and a new flame of love. Mysteriously he became her spiritual father, even though he was much younger than she. John was both loved and feared by many. He suffered terribly the pain of rejection from his religious brothers because he appeared too radical, maybe too loving. He was imprisoned and escaped from prison. This book especially reveals a John in love with Jesus, desirous to follow him in all things, yearning for union with God. John feared and fought against a cheap god, a god of the imagination and of human dreams, a god who was an idol rather than a reality, a god who blesses our mediocrity and weaknesses rather than calling us to growth. John sought the real God, the flame of love that burns and quenches the deepest yearnings of our wounded hearts.

The God revealed by John is not a God to be feared: God is a Lover. Jesus, the Word made flesh, is a gentle and demanding Bridegroom: we are the bride. God seeks us like the Hound of Heaven, to bring us poor mortals into the friendship and ecstasy of love. Iain Matthew shows us through the writings of John, the beauty, the power, the humility and the vulnerability of this wondrous God of Love who is looking for space in our hearts: 'Open up the door of your hearts. Let this Lover, this Tremendous Lover, into your being.' That is the message of John.

Opening up can, however, be painful. It means becoming vulnerable, leaving and losing things that give security. John tells us that the way to open up is through faith. It is through belief and trust in the promises of Jesus, in the person of Jesus, calling us through the pain to a union of love. And John tells us not to seek the marvellous, the extraordinary, or even the charismatic, but rather the presence of God who burns us, who gives and reveals divine love, the life of the Trinity, through faith, hope and through all our gestures of love towards our brothers and sisters, especially the poorest.

For thirty years I have been living in community with people who have learning disabilities. They have led me gently into the mystery announced by Jesus: 'Whosoever welcomes one of these little ones, in my name, welcomes me, and whosoever welcomes me, welcomes the one who sent me' (Luke 9:54). It is a painful, beautiful mystery. And life in l'Arche is both painful and beautiful. It is not always easy to live with people in whom there is much anguish and pain. Yet it is beautiful to live with such people who trust and give their hearts. They reveal the Word who became flesh. But to live this gift or mystery we too are called to believe in Jesus and in his promises; to trust him and to give space in our hearts for his gift.

This book has been important for me and I think will be important for many others. With the help of John of Pain and the pain of John, it leads us to Emmanuel, the God who walks with us. It leads us through the gentleness of Bethlehem to the horror and pain of the Garden of Gethsemane and Golgotha. It leads us to the risen Jesus who says 'peace to you'. It leads us through the paradox of the flame that burns in pain to the flame that burns in love; O delicious wound – the flame that liberates and brings a deep inner peace and joy.

For some people, John of the Cross, the John of Pain and of Ecstasy, seems too austere and complicated: for others he seems too pantheistic, not sufficiently Christ-centred. Iain Matthew reveals beautifully the true John, firmly centred in Jesus, in love with Jesus, the John who through all his life and teaching shows the path to inner liberation and union with God. This book will help many to be God-centred, Jesus-centred, and in all things centred in love.

Jean Vanier
L'ARCHE
60350 Trosly-Breuil
France
March 1995

# PART I – ENTRY

## 1: Impact

John of the Cross speaks to people who feel unable to change. We may have sensed in our lives a call to freedom, to wholeness, to more than what we are now. John felt this as a call to reach out for God. But within us, an unvoiced fear can make change impossible. It is the fear that when we reach, we may not find. It begs the question: if I give myself, will God fill me in my life?

Our being naturally hesitates to say 'yes' to a one-way track that may end only in wasteland. This is the undermining fear, and while we may not opt for a different track, we may never fully choose this one.

Here John of the Cross has something helpful to say. Poet, pastor, mystic, John is first a witness to the impact of God in his life. He has taken the risk of surrender, and can speak with the authority of one who has been there. He testifies to a God who, precisely, is pressing in to meet, to change, and to fill us in our deepest need.

John's language is moulded to echo this impact. He wrote strongly in verse: his God is poetry, and only weakly prose. He wrote in the idiom of bride and bridegroom – the least inadequate image for the way he understands his God to be.

In the following pages, we aim to catch the echo of that impact, not so much to review John's writings as, through his writings, to sound his soul. We aim to recover there his witness to a self-bestowing God. Love changes people, and John's witness to God's love may help us to trust and to be brave.

There is a second point. A generous God is fine when things are running smoothly. But what when they are not and darkness is invading? What when trusted patterns have broken down, or we feel too far gone to bother even trying? We dwell at outer limits, and some events in life – loss, failure, stress, sin – remind us of the threat of chaos.

2 *The Impact of God*

## Places and dates in John's life

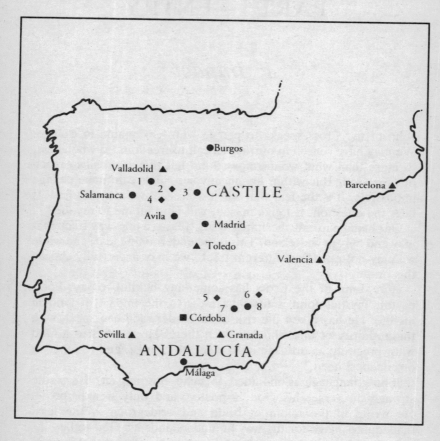

- ● Population 10,000-25,000
- ■ Population 25,000-50,000
- ▲ Population over 50,000
- ◆ Other centres

1  Medina del Campo
2  Arévalo
3  Segovia
4  Fontiveros
5  La Penuela (La Carolina)
6  Beas de Segura
7  Baeza
8  Ubeda

1551: taken to live in Medina del Campo, receives some schooling, and begins work as a nurse
1563: enters the Carmelite Order in Medina
1564: studies as a Carmelite in Salamanca
1567: ordained priest, meets Teresa of Avila
1568: initiates Teresa's reform among the friars
1572: working with Teresa in Avila
1577: in December, John is captured, taken to Toledo and imprisoned
1578: August, escapes from Toledo, and heads south
1578–82: ministry near Beas, then in the university town Baeza
1582–8: ministry in Granada – the years of writing, administration, travel
1588: returns to Castile, to Segovia, for quieter years of ministry
1590: disagreements within the Order begin to affect John's position
1591: John prepares to embark for Mexico, under a cloud of slander; a time of solitude in La Peñuela, then to Ubeda, where he dies on 13/14 December.

That is where John of the Cross stands: at the threshold of uncertainty; and he assures us that what dwells beyond is not simply chaos. The darkness bears the Spirit of God, who broods over the waters of death and has power to work a resurrection.

That is the second aim of this book: to hear John as he follows the consequences of his vision of God through to those outer regions where God seems absent.

There is a third aim. John's experience of impact and of darkness is in itself no guarantee that our own lives are open to the divine. Scripture knows of only one Way; only if John's word speaks to us of Jesus could it claim to be valid for all.

In sounding John's soul, it is Christ we are seeking. The hope is that we shall find Christ there, giving shape to the universe. In fact, John sees the world slung between Friday and Sunday – a dying and rising where all have a home. In our darkness, he finds Jesus's darkness; and what he echoes is the impact of Easter.

John's experience of Jesus – who was once pinned down, and is now set free – should give us courage when we try to believe in the possibility of change.

To reach this point, we shall go in stages. One step will be to find John's most personal word about God, what he would say if he could speak only once (Part II). Then we must see what meaning that gives to our journey and its darkness (III–IV). This will open up for us the possibility of encounter with God, in faith, and prayer, and lead us to perceive the presence in all this of Jesus (V).

First, however, for John's witness to be valid at all, it has to come from his life. That is the first question: when John speaks, where is he coming from, and whom is he addressing? We shall look at his early life, then at his ministry, as a way into his mind and heart.

# 2: Echoing the Impact

Does John of the Cross know what we are talking about when we tell him of the shadowy areas of our lives? Has he been to those outer limits, where things break down? The question is real. John's writings are cohesive enough in themselves, but their relation to his own history, or to our own complexity, can at times be hard to see.

In life, he was known as a 'quiet man'; where his experience of God was concerned, he was 'slow to speak about such things'.[1] So too in his books: the word 'I' occurs rarely. While the pages clearly present magnificent theory, one could be forgiven for wishing he had spiced the odd page with a personal anecdote.

The anonymity is deceptive. The truth is that John's writing emerges precisely from his history, and at the point of his greatest weakness. It is the fruit of his experience, and so when we come to him, bearing our own experience we can hope to be welcomed. We want to look at that in this chapter.

A first indication of John's being 'in touch' is the readiness with which people approached him. John died at the age of forty-nine, in 1591. For thirty years he had trained and ministered as a priest in the Carmelite Order of friars. In that ministry, people found him attractive.

One instance is the two young hospital attendants who had been asked to accompany him (at this stage sick and debilitated) on a journey across Spain. They had no vested interest in liking him, but on returning to their work-place they asked who he was and 'gave thanks to God for having got to know him and accompanied him.'[2]

So too the servant girl Juana: she found in John a life-long support. When she was an old woman, long after John's death, she still treasured a tiny locket containing his portrait. His letters still spoke to her, especially at times of bewilderment: 'But nothing is failing you . . . The person who desires nothing but God does not walk in darkness, however poor and dark she may be in her own sight . . .'[3]

The friars with whom he lived in community described him recurrently as 'kindly'. He was said to be 'joyful and easy with everyone'.[4] These testimonies do have the glow of hindsight, and John was not given to unrestrained guffawing. But he does seem to have been characterised by a glad serenity:

'His face and appearance conveyed joy and peace. I never saw him moody, or frowning at himself or at his subjects. His behaviour [. . .] was always gentle.'[5]

It sounds lovely; but it was not simply the fruit of a happy disposition. John's personality, like his writing, was forged by a conjunction of love and pain. He was born into a superpower Spain afflicted by widespread poverty and deep discriminations. For the losers in that post-medieval world, existence was fragile, unhygienic, sometimes brutal. If John lived as he did, it was not because he had been sheltered in his youth. He was exposed to life's open wounds, and was formed by that exposure.

Love and pain: the story has it that John's father, Gonzalo de Yepes, a cloth merchant from Toledo, fell in love with Catalina, an orphaned girl who made some kind of living by her weaving in the small trade-route town of Fontiveros. They married, but Gonzalo was disinherited for betraying, as the Yepes family saw it, his roots and his status. In 1542, their third son, John, was born – into a family that was already experiencing the cost of generosity.

In the red-bricked church in Fontiveros a granite slab marks Gonzalo's grave; he fell victim to the shortages which overwhelmed many in mid-century central Spain. His widow, Catalina, with twelve-year-old Francisco, younger Luis, and baby John, was forced to take to the roads in search of better conditions. There followed abortive pilgrimages to the Yepes households around distant Toledo – and the death of the second son. The remaining threesome migrated to Arévalo, then to Medina del Campo, commercial centres in Castile, in the hope that the wool trade might provide sufficient work.

In short, John had a highly destabilised childhood. He grew up at the precarious bottom of a status-conscious society. But it was a poverty made fruitful by the tenderness and defiant mettle of his mother. Work, survival, and welcome seem to have been family watchwords, as they shared with people more destitute than themselves.

John was nine when they arrived in Medina, the major market centre in Castile. The city attracted commerce from northern Europe and from the East, as well as from the peninsula itself. It also attracted disease. John, who had been found a place in an institute for disadvantaged children, transferred in his teens to work as a nurse-cum-porter in one of the city's hospitals, a hospice specifically for people suffering from syphilis. His impressionable adolescent years were spent, then, in the company of people dying from sexually-transmitted disease, an environment, again, of pain, but one which the young man was able to meet with a certain robustness and kind feeling, judging from his sensitivity to the sick which became proverbial in later years.

This accounts for almost half of John's life. When he later came to write, all that experience of love and pain stood behind him.

Teresa of Avila stood behind him too. It was she who helped him to resolve the major crisis of direction in his life.

At twenty-one he had decided his future: he left the hospital to join a community of Carmelite friars. This movement traces its roots back to a group of hermits on Mount Carmel in Israel. On moving west to Europe in the thirteenth century they came to the major cities, professing a life of prayer, brotherhood and ministry, under the patronage of the Virgin Mary 'of Mount Carmel'. As the young nurse considered their way of life in Medina, he presumably perceived in it an invitation to a deeper, more universal kind of love.

After an introductory year, John was sent to the Carmelite college in the bubbling university city of Salamanca, where, three years later, he was ordained priest. But he was dissatisfied. The Order, at least as he had come to know it, had failed to meet his need. Perhaps, as he compared the red-raw reality of his family and his hospital days with the point-scoring and one-upmanship of the university world, he found himself saying, 'This is just not real.' Whatever the reason, he was ready to leave the Carmelite brothers for a more solitary, rigorous kind of life.

It was at this point that he met the decidedly real Teresa de Jesús. She had begun in Avila a reform among the women of the same Carmelite Order, and the movement was beginning to spread: communities small enough to be united, poor enough to be free, committed to seeking God's friendship in prayer, as a way of helping to heal a world 'on fire'.[6] The fifty-two-year-old foundress had come to Medina to establish the second of her convents – anxious too to involve male Carmelites in the project.

Teresa naturally inspired trust. 'They have such blind confidence in me – I don't know how they can do such things!'[7] Like the centre of an earthquake, she was soon to exercise influence across Spain. She and her nuns, who, she maintained, only wanted to pray and to get on with their spinning, seemed an attraction or an irritant that could not be ignored.

John was more of a volcano, rocky on the outside, and passionately ablaze at the core. When she met him, Teresa saw in the diminutive friar one who shared her spirit. 'Your reverence should speak with this man', she was soon to write to a friend. 'Even though he is small [*chico*], I understand him to be huge in the eyes of God.'[8] She invited him to join her reform.

For his part, John found in Teresa one in whom ideals became actual – a commitment to Christ without padding or protection. Youthfully, he said to her, Yes, so long as I don't have to wait long.[9]

In a gentle way, Teresa and John became close. They understood each other. When he left for the south of Spain, she was to write, 'You won't believe how lonely I feel without him.'[10] At the same time she found in him someone who could stand his ground despite her infectious personality. When she was first initiating him into her model of religious life, they disagreed on various points, 'and sometimes', she admits, 'I got annoyed at him'![11]

The two were together again a few years later (1572–4). Teresa had been asked to put order into a highly disordered convent in her native Avila. The convent housed upwards of 130 nuns, held loosely together by walls and some prayers, but horribly distant in much else. Some were well-to-do, with their suites of rooms and even servants; others were destitute. The institution was becoming a skeleton without much inside.

To help her to put something inside, Teresa requested John as chaplain. His reputation for holiness was growing, and his arrival was resented, seen as one more attempt to make the nuns something they had never pretended to be. But they soon perceived wisdom in Teresa's selection. The witnesses testify:

'He [John] bore their imperfections, however many times he might point them out, and he led them forward, at their own imperfect pace, to perfection, without violence, and by weak means led them to strength. And by this mildness and prudent patience of his, he obliged them more than ever.'[12]

When John first met Teresa, he was inexperienced in his ministry. She helped to form him; he was forming her. Commitment and warmth were again combining to make him what he was.

John's word issued out of all of that: a youth forged by love and pain; a religious life maturing under the influence of tensions and fresh vision. But when he finally came to write, his life had funnelled to a fine point which almost had to say *this* word in just this way.

Teresa's renewal was bound to brew trouble. It was inevitably felt as a criticism by those not wishing to join her. The ineptitude of some of her friars did not help; and there were wider political issues, as this Castilian reform, championed by King Philip, clashed with reforming efforts in the Order as a whole, backed by Rome.

The pent-up animosity was off-loaded suddenly in 1577, with John of the Cross as target. On a cold night in early December, his chaplaincy in Avila was raided. The young man was taken away for interrogation and chastisement. Then he disappeared.

On hearing of this arrest by friars opposing her reform, Teresa feared the worst. She wrote to King Philip: 'I would be happier if [he] had fallen into the hands of Moors – they might show [him] more pity.'[13] But for once her personality failed to produce results. Unknown to his friends, John was being taken across the freezing Sierra Guadarrama, to the city of Toledo. There he was incarcerated first in a jail, then in a tiny closet, with little or no light, and left.

Toledo can be very cold in winter, asphyxiating in summer. For John, solitary confinement was to mean malnutrition, regular flogging (causing wounds which stayed with him for years), putrid clothing, and lice. With this went a kind of psychological torture. His captors apparently feigned conversation at the door of his cell, leaving their phrases to foment in his mind. They hinted that he would get out in a coffin. They said the reform – his life's work – had fallen apart.

All this does seem to have affected John's mind. As he ate his scant ration, he had to cope with the fear that it was poisoned.

He had to cope too with the constant insinuation (the walls of his dungeon told him this if nobody else did) that he was a rebel – he, whose religious culture was built on obedience. And he confessed that what pained him deeply was the worry that Teresa and the others would think he had deserted them.[14]

It was all happening together: physical and emotional abuse; a whirl of anxiety in his mind; and, in his relationship with God, darkness. At the time when, if ever, he needed to feel the divine presence, his God seemed distant, even alien, and John felt himself a stranger. His later writings will bear out what contemporary witnesses suspected: 'During the time they had him in prison, he suffered great inner dryness and affliction';[15] 'at times [the Lord] withdrew and left him in inner darkness along with the darkness' of his cell.[16]

Here John was a child. He had been hauled beyond the threshold of his own resources, taken to those outer limits where the only alternatives are a Spirit who fills, or chaos. It was as if the anaesthetic which normal life provides had worn off, his inner self had been scraped bare, and he now ached in a way he never had before for a God who was utterly beyond him. This was the real wound, and it drew from him a raw cry, 'Where are you?'

> *¿Adónde te escondiste . . .?*
> Where have you hidden
> Beloved, and left me groaning?
> You fled like a stag
> having wounded me;
> I went out in search of you, and you were gone.

This is the first stanza of the *Canticle*, one of the poems which the prisoner composed in his dungeon. Astonishingly, it was here, in these circumstances, that his mature writing began.

His later books are all commentaries on his poetry. They unfold the poems and draw us back to them, and through them to the crucible that forged them. To hear his word is, then, a precious privilege. When he finally speaks, this 'quiet man' takes us, from prose, through poetry, into his most personal experience, when his life was most precarious, and his God was a surprise.

After nine months of imprisonment, John escaped. The alternative was death, given his rate of debilitation. In the small hours, after days of painstaking observation, a combination of nerve, ingenuity and loosened screws got him out of his cell; then through a window down knotted strips of sheet, on to a wall and into a courtyard. From there he made his faltering way through the city to the shelter of the Teresian nuns. His appearance was shocking. He later noted whimsically, 'I've been flogged more than Saint Paul!'[17]

Even so, physical escape was not, for John, the ultimate issue. What happened in Toledo was larger than the human conflict which occasioned it. Legally, John was not the most significant target among the reformed friars. His comrades could in fact carry on quite well without him, judging from Teresa's exasperated plea, 'I don't know why it is that nobody ever seems to remember this saint!'[18] Besides, if one removes some of the unnecessary brutality, his punishment was standard for recalcitrant friars, according to ecclesiastical legislation of the time.

Yet more was at stake than the human conflict. John himself was to interpret this episode as a sharing in the sign of Jonah – 'swallowed by the whale', he described it in a letter.[19] When he later wrote of the deepest transformation that God works in a person (the night of the spirit), he used the same terms.

It is as if 'she were swallowed by some sea beast, and felt herself being digested in its lugubrious belly . . . It is a blessing for her to be in this sepulchre of dark death, for the resurrection of the spirit for which she hopes.'[20]

Three days in the belly of the earth: that was the meaning he gave to his imprisonment. He was being granted a share in the dying and rising of Jesus.

Although he escaped, his resurrection was not his escape; he had already come to life before his friends could set about restoring him. The poetry he composed in prison is a sign that something was released in him there which had not been available to him before. The verses convey, not only raw hunger, but also a gift which filled the hunger. When years later he wrote about his *Canticle*, he called it the fruit of 'love, in mystical understanding'.[21] His poems were born not just of genius, but of encounter – of encounter, he says, with Christ, and of what Christ gave him there to 'know' and to 'feel' and to 'desire'.[22]

'Where have you hidden . . .?' In that different kind of poverty, where language seemed no longer to function, it was Christ's visitation that he received, with the eyes of a child and the freshness of Easter morning. He put it this way:

> My beloved, the mountains,
> lonely wooded valleys,
> rare islands,
> thundering rivers,
> the whisper of love, carried by the breeze.
>
> The tranquil night
> at one with the rising dawn,
> the silence of music,
> the mighty sound of solitude
> the feast where love makes all new. (*Canticle A* 13–14).

What kind of visitation? John can speak of an encounter with the divine which takes one's breath away.[23] But he relishes more a presence that emerges from within, from behind; as if one entered a dark room, and sat there on one's own . . . then, after some minutes, yes there is someone there, has always been, a silhouette becoming clear. There, 'in the midst' of obscurity, John speaks of 'a kind of companionship and inner strength which walks with the soul and gives her strength'[24] – a presence that is gentle, imperceptible, 'dark', which evaporates if John tries to describe it but which sustains his life. That is the visitation.

At first glance, then, John's writing seems anonymous. But once we start probing, it appears that all he says – white hot in poetry, cooled down and shared out in prose – he says because he knows it from the inside. His works are autobiography, of an almost too personal kind.

In listening to John, we are hearing an original word. He is not the only one to have said it – the word is as old as Easter. It is not the creation of his ingenuity – he submitted to the word in abject poverty. But he is original in saying it because it claimed him unreservedly and issues from him as his. In his darkness, there was disclosed to him Christ's unpaid-for desire to love him. A God who gives himself, to the poor: that pattern will explain all John has to say.

# 3: Picking Up the Echo

First impressions were not always John's forte. After his escape
from Toledo, he made his way to the southern province of
Andalucia. He reached Beas de Segura, a bright, white town in
the foothills of the sierra, where, three years before, Teresa had
inaugurated one of her communities. The nuns there found the
ex-convict still weak and faltering. They were glad to have him with
them, but there was some irritation when this thirty-six-year-old
referred to their saintly foundress as 'my daughter'. One of the
sisters wrote to Teresa, mentioning the unhappy phraseology,
and asking still for a decent spiritual guide. Teresa's reply was
rather direct:

> 'I was amused, daughter, at your complaint: how unfounded it
> is! Don't you have *my father* there, John of the Cross? He is
> a man whose home is in heaven, full of God. I can assure you
> that since he went down there, I have found no one like him
> in all Castile . . . The sisters should open their souls to him –
> they will see how much good it does them.'[1]

Teresa seems to have known John's gift for empathy. The pain
and affection that had moulded him had also endowed him with
an extraordinary capacity to enter the heart of the other, and
understand it.

This is a second preliminary for us. The first is the assurance that
his word came from experience; the second, that this experience
gave him access to others at their point of need.

There are some striking instances of this. A gentleman named
Francisco de Paz was on the run after having set fire to, of all
things, a convent in Salamanca. Suddenly his life had turned into
a nightmare: he fled to the south of Spain and sought asylum in
a Carmelite community. For a time John was prior of the house,

and, whatever lay behind the crime, he welcomed Francisco and treated him as one of the community. The fugitive later recalled how the friar had 'cheered him, brightened his spirits, and given him a feel for God'. He helped Francisco to cope with his turmoil – 'something I could not possibly have done if, under God, the words of advice and example of this holy man were not there before me.'[2]

Another incident, related by one of John's closest associates, Juan Evangelista, involved a young woman in Avila. She had apparently fallen in love with John, and since he showed no sign of responding, she eventually made her passionate way into his house. Evangelista gives two accounts of how John reacted. In one, he says that John managed to get her out of the house, and that he often told Evangelista that this was the most dangerous situation he had ever been in, because she was very attractive. In the other account, he says that John 'with his usual patience' was able to talk to her about what she was doing and get her to see that it was wrong. 'And she returned the way she had come [jumping over a wall] and went home.' The incident suggests John's humanness, his humaneness to her, and his friendship with Evangelista who says that 'he used to talk with me very openly'.[3]

Fugitives and interlopers apart, John was known as a listener. He was said to 'disapprove of those masters who spend all their time lecturing their novices, instead of recognising their level and guiding them accordingly'.[4] When he listened, he wished to learn, to share a journey; and so for him a favourite way of teaching was to ask questions and draw the person further along the line of their answers.

Francisca, a sister in the Beas community, says that 'as he was so holy . . .' – one expects something like, 'all he said set us on fire'; but instead she says, 'as he was so holy, it seemed as if every word we spoke to him opened a door for *him* . . .' When John asked Francisca how she prayed, her answer opened for him such a door: 'By gazing on God's beauty', she said, 'and rejoicing that he has it'. This resonated with something in John's spirit, and from it he composed more verses – 'Rejoicing, let us go, beloved, our eyes meeting in your beauty . . .' (*Canticle A* stanzas 35–9).[5] John could create because he could learn; he was co-pupil, not simply master.

Sensitivity to the other person characterised John because, in his view, it characterises God. He could say it confidently, even in a culture where religious uniformity was highly prized. To spiritual guides who might want to put people in boxes, he says that 'God carries each person along a different road, so that you will scarcely find two people following the same route in even half of their journey to God.'[6]

No two people follow the same route, because each person is unique and God is infinitely varied. This flexibility is fundamental to John, even though at times his own systems and schemas may be more obvious.

The flexibility is fundamental because it alone does justice to the dignity of each person, a 'most beautiful and finely wrought image of God'.[7] It does justice too to the laws of growth. Growth, though it has its crises, is gradual. So John says that humanity, and each person, was wedded to Christ when he died on the cross, a wedding made ours at our baptism. But that all happens 'at God's pace, and so all at once'. It has to become ours at our pace, 'and so, little by little'.[8]

This, John believes, is God's teaching method: to give himself in a way the person can handle. Why does God give people experiences they may later have to leave behind? Because, he says, God treats us 'with order, gentleness, and in a way that suits the soul'.[9]

Dialogue, respect, 'little by little', 'in a way that suits the soul' – John evidently intends to address lives that are each different, and mostly incomplete. He asks to be read accordingly. In giving a commentary on his prison verses, he says that he wants to offer only 'some general light'.

> 'And I think that this is better. Where words are born of love, it is better to leave them open, so that each person can benefit from them in their own way and at their own spiritual level – this, rather than tying the verses down to a meaning that not everyone could relish.'[10]

In his poetry John is entrusting to us his heartbeat, and inviting us to let it beat with our own. It is a very personal meeting.

His prose works can seem less personal. They can seem to exclude many of us. In some, he is addressing his own Carmelite brothers and sisters. But his most exalted work (the *Living Flame*) is addressed to a lay woman in charge of a household, and his letters spread his teaching to people from various walks of life. More of a problem, perhaps, is his focus on a specific crisis of growth, in which prayer is moving from detail, to simplicity. This may not be everybody's experience. However, there are reasons for not feeling excluded here either.

One reason is that, although John often homes in on this crisis of growth, he frequently throws out lines to bring in readers at different stages on the journey. So he looks forward to further growth (ultimately, to heaven); and he looks back to earlier stages, to the time the person began to take God seriously, back farther to God's efforts to lure her to himself, back to the moment when she came to be, 'flying from the ark of God's almighty power'.[11]

More importantly, what takes place in that crisis of growth is a symptom of the way God is throughout our journey.

If we looked up at the night sky and saw a shooting star, we could react in various ways. One way would be to say, 'Oh look, there is a shooting star'. That would be true, but would not get us very far. Another would be to come to a recognition: 'Oh look – the universe is mobile!' That would also be true, and very significant.

So with John: when he focuses on something outside our immediate experience, various reactions are open to us. One is to say, look at what happened to John of the Cross – one more phenomenon to be stored in a mystical museum. Another is to grasp the meaning as well as the phenomenon and to say, Look! This is the way God is; these are the horizons of our journey.

The reality of grace in us – children of God, temple of the Spirit, bride of the Lamb – in the saints we find unfolded.

In turning to John, we are being approached by a saint, and a mystic. As a saint, he was greatly surrendered to the action of God. As a mystic, he experienced that action as, in some sense, manifest. His sanctity holds out to us the Christian project: to come to want what God wants. His 'experience' heralds divine freedom – free to act openly, free to act hiddenly, displaying beauty in infinite variety.[12]

On those terms, we may not be so saintly – God's will and ours may strike notes of discord. Nor so mystical – God's action may impinge less upon our awareness. But it is of vital concern to know that what took place in John discloses what is real in us, albeit in embryo and in hiding.

That is John's greatest gift: not so much to tell us what to do, nor to pinpoint our place on the map, but to draw back the curtains and disclose the whole journey as real.

John has, then, a word for us which is relevant and sensitive. But it is also urgent. If his writing is on fire at his end, the flame of his own experience, it catches fire again at our end, as he sees our potential. Where prose was concerned, he was a reluctant writer. He wrote at others' insistence ('responding to the questions they put . . .'[13]) and on account of their need: not because of 'any ability I might see in myself for such an arduous task, but because of the confidence I have in the Lord, confidence that he will help me to say *something*, on account of the great need of many people . . .'[14]

John lived in an age which was well-fed with religiosity. There was no shortage of religious material, but John did perceive a short-age of depth. His concern is not to add to the material, but to help people connect with the vitality concealed in what is already there. He writes of people who load themselves up with extraordinary practices, and get nowhere; 'if they were careful to put half the effort' in the right place, it would yield more in a month than otherwise in years.[15] That is the aim: not to extract yet more effort, but to open the path to what will genuinely meet the needs.

His own story had sensitised him to those needs. He had felt them himself, and it made matters quite simple. For John, there is only one goal. His word for it is not so much 'perfection' – as if it were only about me becoming myself; he prefers to call it 'union' – 'union with God', the 'union of love'. He chose the word deliberately: people speak of 'perfection, which here we are calling union of the soul with God'.[16] His entire enterprise pounds along in a relentless quest: that this person should be filled with this God. Life remains dispersed till this God is at its centre.

Whether or not she realises it, the human person aches for such a union: 'It was to reach this that he created her in his image and likeness'; it is for this that we are 'always hungering, by our very nature, and by the gift of God'; 'nothing less' than this will 'satisfy the heart'. 'In short, it was for this goal of love that we were created'.[17]

In saying this, John is not merely analysing the species. He is recognising a real possibility. He sees it as a live issue, and feels 'sorrow and pity' where people ignore it;[18] sorrow, pity, and a certain disbelief: 'Oh souls created for this greatness and summoned to it – what are you doing?!'[19]

In these chapters we have met a quiet man sharing with us his own history, and anxious to speak into ours. We are in place now to hear the word he speaks. In approaching him, we know he will not steamroller us. But we know too that his word is demanding, because he has sounded our potential for greatness and does not want to see us short-changed. His urgency can be unnerving.

What excludes us from his writing, however, is not our being too low down some scale of perfection. For John, the point of departure is a sense of need, a recognition ('falling into the realisation') that our life will not be complete till God is at its centre.[20] This had galvanised him into writing in his Toledo dungeon; into writing, and into further seeking: 'Where . . .? I went out in search of you, and you were gone.'

We are excluded, not by where we are, but by an unwillingness to go farther. We are welcomed in when we wish to seek, to change, to be changed. We can hear John's answer if we can share his question:

'Beloved, where have you hidden?'

# PART II – Gift

## 4: A Quiet Man Speaks

'God is love.' It is easy to say it. But we also know of hard words, a Christ who speaks of Cross and narrow gates, who demands a dying, his tongue a two-edged sword and his eyes on fire. How does this God, not just the kindly God, but the living God, feel about the flesh and blood, sin and beauty of our world? The theory of God's universal love is clear; but the question tends to be more actual and specific. Where do I, insignificant and complex, stand in relation to the All-Holy?

We are turning to John because his answer has authority. He was exposed to the divine approach, and his word issued from it. We now have to find the place in which he delivers to us his experience of God in its most concentrated form. Much of his writing is directive, pastoral; but our quest is for the original impact which set all that in motion.

We find it in his work, the *Living Flame*. This – poem and commentary – would be John's desert island book, the writing he would keep if all but one book had to be discarded. Before looking at what he says in it, we want first to draw out this fact that here we have John at his most personal.

After his escape from captivity and journey south to Andalucia, John began to add to and share his prison poetry. His brother and sister Carmelites set themselves to learn his poems and put them to music. His stanzas even reached Teresa, back in the north, who was delighted to hear them sung. They asked the poet to do the impossible and explain some of the verses. He put some of his comments down on paper.

He was also writing cards and letters of spiritual direction, something he had already done in his Avila days (1572–7). As one sister there nostalgically recalled: 'He had a gift for consoling those who came to him, by his words and in the cards he wrote. I

received some myself – also some jottings about spiritual matters.
I would dearly love to have them now.'[1]

In time, comments and notes gave way to four continuous
commentaries: *Canticle*, on the prison poem, 'Where have you
hidden?'; *Ascent* and *Night* on his most famous poem, 'One dark
night'; and the commentary on his hymn to the Holy Spirit, the
*Living Flame*.

Each of the four works has a different emphasis, and a different
style. We shall see the emphases in succeeding chapters. As for
style, *Ascent* is more of a treatise, on Christian growth; *Night* is
descriptive, portraying that growth at its most painful; *Canticle* is
lyrical, sometimes allegorical, where growth is a lovers' journey of
search and encounter. However, it is the *Flame* that stays closest
of all the commentaries to the poetic impulse. There are sections of
practical guidance; but most paragraphs just let the verses unfold
their compacted meaning, each poetic image rippling out across
the page. This is John at his most relaxed, able thus to be most
intense. It is a song of wonder, and is not really 'for' anything,
other than itself.

One sign that the *Flame* is John's most personal work is his
supreme confidence in writing. He recognises that some readers
may be bemused, others incredulous, but he shows no sign of
playing down what he is saying.[2]

He was confident enough to write the book at speed, despite
his work-load. The decade following his Toledo experience was
the busiest of his life. After setting up a Carmelite college in the
charismatic university town of Baeza (1579–82), he was transferred
to Granada, where the friars had a community next to the beautiful
Moorish palace overlooking the city. The views are magnificent.
'Give him alms lady', a graffito there pleads on a blind beggar's
behalf, 'for life knows no sorrow like being blind in Granada'. This
was John's home for the next six years.

As said, he was busy: he travelled an estimated 8,600 miles
during that time, a total notched up particularly during his term as
Superior of Teresa's convents and monasteries in southern Spain
(1585–7). As a letter of June 1586 announces, 'God is giving us so
much to do these days that we cannot keep up with it all!'[3]

It was in these improbable circumstances that he wrote the
*Flame* (sixty small-print pages in the modern edition). As his
friend Evangelista reports, he produced it 'while he was Vicar
Provincial, at the request of Doña Ana de Peñalosa. He wrote

it during a very busy fortnight which he spent here in this house [Granada].'[4]

Written between calls in a spare fortnight, the whole work seems to have unfolded at the speed of an inspiration.

As well as confidence, the work was born in an atmosphere of trust. The Doña Ana just mentioned came to know John when he first arrived in Granada. He was accompanying a group of eight nuns who were hoping to inaugurate a convent there. On arrival they found that the Archbishop was unwilling to give permission, and that the offer of property had been withdrawn, leaving the nuns with their good intentions and nowhere to live. Ana offered them her own house. Although the prelate soon acquiesced (helped along by a lightning storm which set his library on fire), suitable property came more slowly; the life-line which Ana had thrown to the nuns had to stretch for several months.

During this period John visited Ana's guests. Ana found in him a guide who could help to give meaning to the sorrow throbbing inside her, since the deaths, three years earlier, of her husband and only daughter.

John for his part could write to Ana as to a close friend, especially during the persecutions that darkened the last year of his life. In one letter from this period he promises to remember her brother, who was being ordained a priest: 'Forgetful though I may be, he is so close to his sister, *whom I keep always in my mind*, that I won't be able to forget him either.'[5]

John dedicated the *Flame* to her: evidently, limpid trust made possible a genuine sharing.

Trust was there again at the end. 'Tomorrow I'm off to Ubeda to get over a touch of fever,' John confided in September 1591 (five years after *Flame* had been written).[6] The 'touch of fever' marked the onset of erysipelas which was soon to inflame the friar's entire body. The surgeon was called in. As he lanced and cauterised rotting flesh, his treatment really amounted to well-intentioned torture. But the man was trying, and in trying he came to know John in a unique way. Gratefully, the patient gave him a manuscript. It contained the *Living Flame*. It is as if John was entrusting him with his last bequest to the world.

Along with this confidence and trust, the *Flame* has an inner consistency, a third sign that here John is at home.

Any discussion of experience, particularly one's experience of God, is going to feel inadequate. Talking about an event is, after

all, talk; – the word 'fire' never burnt anybody. Nevertheless, in
the *Flame*, the dissonance between word and reality is reduced
to a minimum. For John at least, the vitality inside him scorches
the paper he touches. 'Transformed in love's fire', 'blazing in its
flame'[7] – the language can be hard to take, and he trusts us not
to take it wrongly, but it seems to have been John's only way
of being true to himself. And he waited until he could be true:
'To speak of the depths of the spirit, one has to return to those
depths.' He confesses to having felt aversion to commenting on
the poem 'till now, when the Lord does seem to have drawn back
the veil and bestowed some warmth'.[8] By his own admission, his
prayer, his poem (expressing the prayer), and his prose (unfolding
the poem) glow with consistent heat. His words here bring us as
close as words can to the reality of his relationship with God, the
'depths of the spirit', 'unveiled'.

A final sign that *Flame* portrays experience is the way in which
words are flexed and eventually left behind. The whole work was
composed some years after Toledo – when love had had time, John
says, to reach a 'much deeper quality'.[9] He has crossed further
frontiers, into human and divine realms which he admits are new to
him, and language must be stretched to cope with new demands.

So while medieval mystics spoke of the inner self as the 'spirit',
the 'centre', the 'depth', John wants to say, 'Yes, but more so'.
He forms new combinations to convey that 'extra': 'in the middle
of the heart of the spirit'; 'the intimate substance of the depth of the
soul'; even the 'infinite centre'.[10] That is the reality, and language
has to be made to obey.

Made to obey, or abandoned: that too is a sign of authenticity.
The language he stretches sometimes snaps, unable to keep up
with the advances of his spirit. Hypotheses can be discussed for
hours; but only the person who has been there will say, 'I will not
deny it, though I cannot explain it'.

'No words have been invented for the works of God in such
souls. The only language to cope with them is acceptance for
oneself, experience, joy and silence.'[11]

The *Flame* ends in this kind of willing defeatism. Of the breath
of God's Spirit 'I would prefer not to speak'; otherwise 'it would
look like something less than it in fact is . . . So, for this reason,
I shall stop here. END.'[12] A rather abrupt finale, and the author

tidied it up in a later version, but he still opted to say less rather than more. As one critic neatly puts it, John's commentaries are 'a failure, foreseen, though magnificent'.[13] Had they 'succeeded', or their author felt satisfied, their content would be suspect.

These are some signs that in the *Flame* John is most himself – confident, close, consistent, and hushed. If so, his witness to God is here least protected, and we are ready to hear this now, first in the poem.

The poem may not appeal to everyone; it may not be 'us'. Although it is sometimes used as a hymn for Pentecost, we may in fact never feel comfortable praying it.

For one thing, there is the language of lover and beloved. The poet shows his indebtedness to secular love poetry here, not afraid to use it to express his relationship with the divine. More, he shows his indebtedness to the traditional understanding of the Song of Songs, as the love song of Yahweh for Israel, of the Lamb for his Church, of Christ for the soul. John's use of marriage imagery is more than a literary conceit. It points to an organic link between human and divine love. As the Scriptures portray it, married love contains within itself a reality beyond itself. It is so sacred that it derives from and points to the love of Christ for humankind. When John of the Cross uses this language, he is owning his place in the Church, the 'chaste bride' wedded to Christ 'her only husband' (2 Cor. 11:2).[14]

Even granted this, we may still not identify with John's poem. But the point here is not so much its usefulness to us, as its testimony to John and his God. The point is that he said it, that *he* said it, and that it is possible to relate to God in this way. When he wants to bear witness, not to the easy God, but to the living God, approaching the 'flesh and blood, sin and beauty of our world', he considers this the least inadequate way to say it.

> *¡Oh llama de amor viva . . .!*
> Flame, alive, compelling,
> yet tender past all telling,
> reaching the secret centre of my soul!
> Since now evasion's over,
> finish your work, my Lover,
> break the last thread, wound me and make me whole!

> Burn that is for my healing!
> Wound of delight past feeling!
> Ah, gentle hand whose touch is a caress,
> foretaste of heaven conveying
> and every debt repaying:
> slaying, you give me life for death's distress.
>
> O lamps of fire bright-burning
> with splendid brilliance, turning
> deep caverns of my soul to pools of light!
> Once shadowed, dim, unknowing,
> now their strange new-found glowing
> gives warmth and radiance for my Love's delight.
>
> > Ah! gentle and so loving
> > you wake within me, proving
> > that you are there in secret and alone;
> > your fragrant breathing stills me,
> > your grace, your glory fills me
> > so tenderly your love becomes my own.'

If this is John's most personal witness to his life and his God, what impression does it give? Probably as many impressions as there are readers. And if John entrusts himself to us in his poetry, he cherishes that personal response of ours.

There is, however, one feature that pervades the poem, almost so obvious that it could be missed. It is this: in the verses, all the initiative belongs to the other.

That is John's most authentic witness to God. When John is most himself, what we find filling his mind is a God who is, supremely, active.

The evidence is simple: the verbs are about what 'you' are doing. You are piercing, repaying, slaying, giving life, waking, breathing; you did seem oppressive, but it was you that seemed it; you may tear the veil, but it has to be you. If 'my' soul gives radiance it is because you shine on it; and if 'I' love it is because your love awakens me.

When John comments on his verses, the pervasive feature is the same. His God anticipates, initiates, gives, transforms; like a flame entering till it engages the 'deepest centre'. John's universe is drenched in a self-outpouring God.

The commentary presents a strange world; to survive it, we must suspend disbelief. Its pages breathe rhapsody. They are peppered with exclamations – 'Oh . . .! How . . .!' – which, the author maintains, mean what they say: 'affection and praise'.[15] In the *Living Flame* John comes wide-eyed, not to explain, but to say thank you.

The work is his 'magnificat'.[16] In one way that makes it harder to follow – the more infectious his wonder, the less informative it is. As someone overhearing Mary's song of praise would realise that something stupendous had happened, but not know what, in the *Flame* John conveys impact more than story. It is for us to flesh out the story; what John does is remind us that the pictures are live.

Live, and therefore open to infinite horizons. The one he encounters is not prissy, stale, or exhausted; his God is new, daring, vital. Flame, fire, blazing, burning – the basic image is meant to say something.

John makes it explicit. Where God is concerned, 'love is never idle; it is in continuous movement'.[17]

The Spirit that John knows is 'an infinite fire of love', able to set the heart 'blazing more intensely than all the fire in the world'.[18]

His presence is 'fiesta' in the soul, 'like a song that is new, always new, wrapped round with joy, and love'.[19]

With such a God, the journey does not narrow into dainty, stuffy elegance; it opens out into broader landscapes, where issues are more real, and more is at stake. Love grows geometrically (two, four, eight, sixteen); it spirals upwards with increasing velocity.[20]

Rapture, and infinite breadth: these characteristics depend on a third, the most fundamental. As the poem throbs with the activity of Another, so, permeating the pages of the commentary, is an awareness of a self-communicating God, a God whose plan is to fill us with nothing less than himself.

This is God's 'language', in which speaking is doing, and his action is himself.[21] The flame is a person, 'the Spirit of your Bridegroom', the breath of Christ. The work pulses with God's eagerness to belong to other persons. Nothing less would satisfy the 'liberality of his generous grace'. He gives, and what he gives is himself.[22]

So John's magnificat responds to a Spirit-flame who does not wait to be approached. He hovers over to enter, presses in, and once in, burns through until he finds the deepest core of the human person.

This had been John's question – 'Where have *you* hidden?' His project hung on this prospect: not just perfection, but union in love. To this his language has been geared: bride and Bridegroom, married intimacy, the Bible's symbol of the Christ who 'loved the church and gave himself' (Eph. 5:25). Now, as we sound John's experience at its most authentic, we find this to be the reality he knew: a God who is pressing in to give *himself*.

He does not give in a general way only, like rays of sunlight shining above a mountain, but leaving me-in-particular shadowed in the valley. John's God enters to confront the person as if there were no other. It seems to her that God has no other concern, 'but that he is all for her alone.'[23] God comes in strength, capable of reconciling opposites, 'giving life for death's distress'. His embrace is as wide as Good Friday to Sunday, and nothing in the person is too much for him. He finds in the soul, not a burden, or a disappointment, but a cause for 'glad celebration'.[24] John dares to place on the lips of his God the words:

'I am yours, and for you, and I am pleased to be as I am that I may be yours and give myself to you.'[25]

If our understanding of the *Flame* is correct, John experienced this as real. He is aware that people may find it too much to cope with, and looks for an explanation. The only one he finds is God himself.

'When a person loves another and does her good, he does her good and loves her with his own personality and character. So with your Bridegroom, who is in you: it is *as he who he is* that he shows you favour.'[26]

As the seal, so the impress; as the flame, so the burn; as the Spirit's desire to give – which 'is great' – so 'great will be the wound'.[27] The measure of God's gift is God's desire to give, and his guarantee is himself.

That is the atmosphere of John's most personal work: it discloses a God who gives, evokes joy and wonder, and who is his own guarantee. Finally, such a God, in giving, transforms.

While it may at times be hard to keep up with John's language, his God at least does not simply overwhelm. His approach creates possibilities. A favourite verb for God's action is 'to make *grande*': 'God's purpose is to make the soul great'.[28] The Spirit does more than arrive. He 'provokes', 'invites', and perseveres in his approach until 'he makes the person wide enough, open enough, and capable of himself'.[29] The Spirit's approach is a master class, not a performance: he shows us how, puts the instrument in our hands, and, holding our hand, plays the tune with us.[30] In giving, God makes us able to receive, and respond.

The *Living Flame* here discloses the greatness of the human person. The fact is that only God is able to uncover aspects of our humanity which otherwise lie fallow. So of the 'deep caverns of the soul', John says that 'nothing less than the infinite will fill them'. This immensity usually (perhaps thankfully) stays hidden – though more hidden than it should be when rubbish is thrown into it. But when these caverns 'are empty and pure, the thirst and hunger and sense of spiritual longing is more than can be borne . . . The capacity of these caverns is deep, because that which they can hold is deep and infinite; and that is God.'[31]

Even the body – ambiguous, sometimes seductive, easily abused – is meant for 'glory', and John sees it already open to the divine. He can speak of the Spirit anointing every limb with joy, 'right down to the last joints in feet and hands'![32] In the divine approach, while much may be cleansed, it seems that nothing is discarded.

For John, Paul's phrase has come alive. He quotes it: 'I live, now not I, but Christ lives in me.'[33] This is resurrection, seen, not just as history, nor solely as reward, but as a process. The first paragraph of *Flame* presents the process succeeding – the person 'utterly bathed now in glory and love, in her inmost core pouring out nothing less than rivers of glory'.[34]

By this stage we may feel somewhat out of our depth. John's word – a self-giving God, lavishing himself upon the world; humanity, besieged by glory – is undeniably extreme. But, in whatever form we find his word accessible, it is vital to hear it. It speaks truth about God and about the human person. Not to hear it would be to leave us short-changed as human beings.

John presents here a strange world, and we shall look next at how it relates to ourselves. But he already deserves gratitude for doing that most Christian thing: witnessing to the resurrection. By sharing his experience of faith, he takes us back to Easter morning and lets us glimpse the impact of the Father upon the heart of the Son:

'Love! Love on fire, lavish, active: you are glorifying me as much as my soul can bear it and hold it.'[35]

# 5: The Gospel Has Eyes

Imagine sitting on a quiet bench in the park, between some flower beds and backed by a hedge . . . composing a quite personal letter, absorbed and writing . . . Someone is there – you notice out of the corner of your eye – someone is there looking at you; and has been for some time . . . What a moment of exposure!

The gospel has eyes – 'the eyes I long for so', John calls them – and the point comes on the journey where the bride meets those eyes which had long been looking on: 'It seems to her that he is now always gazing upon her.'[1] It is a moment of exposure, as she finds herself a factor in another's life and heart. In the *Flame*, John has captured that moment, and delivered it to us. In fact it encompasses our whole existence. We want to highlight this broader significance of John's word in this chapter.

It has been said that 'a person is enlightened', not 'when they get an idea', but 'when someone looks at them'.[2] A person is enlightened when another loves them. The eyes are windows on to the heart; they search the person out and have power to elicit life.

So the gospel has eyes which are not dispassionate, nor merely passive. Their gaze is not an art gallery gaze, wandering from exhibit to exhibit and leaving what they see obviously unchanged. Their gaze engages what they see and affects it: 'For God, to gaze is to love, and to work favours.'[3] These eyes are effective: 'God's gaze works four blessings in the soul: it cleanses the person, makes her beautiful, enriches and enlightens her.'[4]

This statement comes towards the end of the *Canticle* where the author is reviewing his whole journey and thanking God that it was possible at all (stanzas 32–3). It implies a whole way of looking at Christian life. Christianity is an effect, the effect of a God who is constantly gazing at us, whose eyes anticipate, radiate, penetrate and elicit beauty.

You looked with love upon me
and deep within your eyes imprinted grace;
this mercy set me free,
held in your love's embrace,
to lift my eyes adoring to your face (stanza 32).

These gospel eyes are traditionally called 'grace': a God who gives, and whose gift makes us able to respond. John puts the doctrine neatly: 'For God to set his grace in the soul is to make her worthy and capable of his love'.[5] This divine gazing is the foundation of any Christian endeavour – 'without his grace, his grace cannot be merited'.[6] The trouble is that, because it is foundational, because it is as pervasive as the air, this divine initiative can be forgotten, and our religion becomes one more human enterprise, knotty, petty and ultimately suffocating. 'Outside of God', John says, 'everything is narrow'.[7]

The mystics keep alive the sense that the enterprise belongs to God, and so help the air to circulate. The *Living Flame* does this. As a hymn to God's initiative, it reminds us, not of a chance phenomenon, but of a state of affairs. 'I am yours and for you . . .' – this is grace unfolded and writ large. John experienced God's self-giving with 'most enlightened faith' and with the veil 'drawn back'.[8] Yet, he says,

> 'God *is always* like this, as the soul now sees him to be: stimulating, guiding, and giving being and strength and graces and gifts to all creatures, holding them all in himself.'[9]

The *Flame* tapped into an 'always' rooted in God himself: in an eternal bestowing, Father to Son, Son to Father, rapt in the Spirit, and guaranteeing us infinite room to breathe:

> 'The Father spoke one word, who was his Son, and this word he *is always speaking* in eternal silence. It is in silence that the soul must hear it.'[10]

That there is a universe at all is, for John, the evidence of God's involvement. This comes early in the 'Where have you hidden?' song (stanza 5), as an initial response to the bride's search for signs of her Beloved. The created world answers that he did pass this way, clothing whatever he looked at 'with beauty . . .'

'A person is enlightened when someone looks at them.' Chaos
is enlightened when God looks at it. The 'Bridegroom' casts his
gaze across the face of the abyss and sprays life across it. That
is John's amazing understanding of creation: the universe, each
element in it, each event in it, and the web of those events held
together – all thought, all friendship, all history – are given being
by the eyes of Another, eyes 'communicating' being to the world.
Such a creation is flamboyant in its beauty, as the Word of God,
glancing kindly but wildly, 'scatters a thousand graces' and floods
the cosmos with traces of who he is.[11]

There is a marvellous sense here of God's creative act being,
not just a primeval beginning, but a present event. The event is
as gentle, in a sense as precarious, but also as loving as the gaze
of one who cares.

There is a marvellous sense too that the universe has a character
to it. John says that when the Father gazes, he gazes through his
Son. The Son is his face, smiling upon the world. 'God saw that
they were good', which was to make them good by 'seeing them'
in his Son.[12] Creation has a Son-like colour, a Son-like shape which
the Son alone could fill.

That is John's real interest: the Son does undertake to fill us.
His eyes not only hold us in being; they hold us in friendship,
a friendship made possible when he meets us with human eyes.
Humanity is enlightened when the Son becomes flesh, looks at us,
draws us out of ourselves, raises us up to himself. In this the whole
cosmos is renewed.

'This he did when he became man, lifting man up in the beauty
of God, and so lifting up all creatures in him . . . In this raising
up in the Son's incarnation and in the glory of his resurrection
according to the flesh, the Father gave creatures not just a partial
beauty; we can say that he entirely clothed them in beauty and
dignity.'[13]

A God 'whose gaze clothes the world in beauty and joy': that
is how John understands the event of Christ, born and risen,
confirming the universe in what it is meant to be.[14] This is also
the way he interpreted his most personal experience of God in
the *Flame* ('wrapped round with joy and love'). That is the point
here: his mystical experience sits within the mystery of Christ.
That is our place too, however differently it may impinge on us;

so John's word is our word: his message can reawaken us to who we are.

There is a paragraph in the *Flame* which makes this transition from John to ourselves in a powerful way.

The author is commenting on the 'deep caverns of my soul' (stanza 3). He does not want to interrupt the flow of writing, but he decides to do so because what he has to say is so important, 'not only for these people who are doing so well, but also for all the others who are seeking their beloved'.[15] Here, then, he is turning round to include in his scope all who are 'seeking' – all who at some level can share his question, 'Where . . .?'. The statement heads the main pastoral section of the book, on growth in prayer.[16] A lot is at stake, and the author starts off in an unusually magisterial tone: 'I wish to say . . .':

> 'Because it is so necessary, not only for these people who are doing so well, but also for all the others who are seeking their beloved, I wish to say it. In the first place, you should realise that, *if the person is seeking God, much more is her Beloved seeking her.*'

Much more, because first, and farther. That is the message: it is God who is seeking, and God is always seeking. And he intends to pursue his seeking to the very limit:

> 'much more is her Beloved seeking her [. . .] So the soul must understand that *God's desire* in all the good things he does to her [. . .] is to prepare her for further anointings [. . .] more like him in quality, until she comes to such purity, such refined readiness, that she merits union with God . . .'[17]

The gospel has eyes; they reach to the heart, and change it.

## What must we do?

We have probed John's experience at its most personal, in the *Living Flame*. We found there a mind dominated by awareness of an impinging God. Now he is telling us that this is God's character throughout the journey. What response does all this demand?

There will be a call to action; we shall listen to that in the next chapter. But it is action based on an attitude, and the *Flame*, insofar as it looks for a response at all, is concerned with this attitude. The response required is, above all, that we believe.

Believe, namely, that God does want to give us himself; that he is giving us himself and that he means to pursue that gift through to its ultimate consequences.

Belief is John's requirement because that may be all we have to go on: God's gift may not be evident to the mind or feelings. Trust in God's word, and not in evidential security, must be our ultimate guarantee.

John first wrote the *Flame* when, he says, the veil was drawn open.[18] This presumably means that, for him, the veil was normally closed: the action of the Spirit was generally more hidden. In that case, what we call his 'experience' was essentially a reality of faith, and continued to be real even when it was not obvious.

John re-edited the *Flame* at the end of his life in bitter circumstances, including a campaign of libel against him, which do seem to have sunk into his soul. A letter to Ana de Peñalosa gives a hint of this, written from a desert monastery far away from the gathering political storm.

'I'm in excellent form, glory be to God, and things are good. This desert freedom is helping me greatly, soul and body . . . though my soul is faring very poorly. The Lord must want it to go through a desert of its own.'[19]

A desert in John's soul: yet in that, he could reaffirm all that the *Flame* was saying. John's experience of the Spirit was not valued because it was felt; it was valued because it was real, and he could trust its reality even when he could not feel it.

God's action is, simply, deeper: 'reaching the secret centre . . .', the poem says. Absence of insight or feeling – even if it leaves the person 'in dryness, in darkness, feeling abandoned' – does not certify that 'God is any farther away'.[20]

To believe in God's involvement in these circumstances is a huge statement of trust. 'God deliver us from ourselves', John says in one of his letters; 'may he give us what he pleases when *he* so desire'.[21]

So: rely on faith rather than evidence. But that is not the main aspect of the belief required in the *Flame*. The danger envisaged is not so much that we shall trust in the wrong thing, but that we shall stop trusting at all; that, while we may never say it in so many words, we shall cease to believe that we are a factor in God's life.

Survival demands a certain scepticism. We are trained to cope as social beings by keeping our desires within realistic limits. But where God is concerned, the problem lies in our desiring too little, and growing means expanding our expectations; or rather, making his generosity, not our poverty, the measure of our expectations.

'What prepares the soul to be united with God is: the desire for God.'[22] Such faith-desire is the dynamo to John's system. When the goal seems impossibly distant, he does not suggest that we settle for something more manageable. He agrees that it is distant, and says that desire will get us there:

> 'So the soul must desire with all her desire to come to what in this life lies beyond her mind or the capacity of her heart.'[23]

It is here that the sureness of touch, which we saw John display in the *Flame*, comes to the fore. He never backs down from his statement of divine generosity. If he anticipates readers shaking their heads ('He's gone too far this time'), there is no hint of a 'Yes, you're right, let me rephrase that'. There is only a 'Please believe me'.

The prologue to *Flame* already says it. Christ's promise – that he and the Father would come and make their home in those who love him (John 14:23) – determines Christ's gift:

> 'There is no need for astonishment that God should work such [favours] . . . If we consider that he is God, and that he does them as God, with infinite love and goodness, it will not seem beyond the bounds of reason . . .'[24]

The point keeps recurring: 'Do not be astounded'; 'There is nothing incredible in this, if we believe, as we must believe, that . . .'; 'there is no need for astonishment that . . .'[25] He is most forceful in a passage he added in his final edition – as if the objections had grown louder ('Isn't he going too far?'); he, too, wanted to make things clear:

> 'I do not doubt that some people, not understanding this nor knowing the reality of it, will either disbelieve it, or think it exaggerated, or reckon it less than it in fact is . . .'

He pins what he is about to say on his moral authority ('I answer'),
which itself rests on the word of God:

> 'or reckon it less than it in fact is. But to all of these I answer,
> that the Father of lights, whose hand is not shortened, and *who
> pours himself out abundantly*, without partiality, *wherever he
> finds space*, like a ray of sunlight, and joyfully discloses himself
> to people on the footpaths and highways – this God does not
> hesitate or disdain to find his delight among the children of
> men . . .'[26]

That is what the *Living Flame* asks of us: that we do not cease to
believe in God's desire to fill us. This does not mean the hope
that, if I am credulous enough, something magical will happen. It
means rather that this, a lavish God, who does not hesitate, is the
horizon within which I choose to live my life.

This is resurrection faith ('Blessed are those who have not
seen . . .', John 20:29); it depends, not on our receiving a further
appearance of the risen Lord, but on the Lord, who in appearing
then showed himself dependable now. It is faith tensed by desire
(You did not see him, yet 'you love him', 1 Pet. 1:8); desire, not
for a repetition of John's experience of God, but for God, whose
impress on him announces God's vitality now.

'You show yourself first and you go out to meet those who desire
you.'[27] Where the Other loves first, the vital response on our part
is desiring faith – believing that God does love first and that his
love is effective. John prays for that for us, as he comments
on the words of the *Flame*, 'You wake within me.' The prayer
joins the author then and the reader now in the 'always' of a
self-communicating God.

> 'Do you awaken us, my Lord,
> and shed your light upon us
> that we might recognise and come to love
> the blessings that you *always* hold out to us,
> and we shall realise
> that you stepped forward to show us your favour
> and that you have not forgotten us.'[28]

# PART III – Space

## 6: The Right Kind of Emptiness

John of the Cross has been called 'one of the world's great simplifiers'.[1] Once we have sounded the impact of God in his soul, heard most clearly in his *Living Flame*, things start snapping quickly into position. His testimony – to an impinging God, intent on unleashing on the human person the gift of himself – allows us to see the rest of his work in the way he saw it. One can look down what is a majestic tree-lined avenue, instead of coming upon it at a busy intersection in a maze of streets. The journey looks worth while, and possible.

'If the person is seeking God, much more is her Beloved seeking her.'[2] This is the fact, and it requires a fundamental revision in our perceptions of our own roles.

Stranded and starving, somebody has to get packed up and sent off into the unknown to search for food, taking what water is left, hacking a way through the undergrowth, hoping somehow to forge a path to something somewhere. But then comes the noise of a helicopter, and rescue approaching. That changes everything. The one thing needed now is some space, so that what is coming can come.

This is the revision: for John, God is an approaching God, and our main job will be not to construct but to receive; the key word will be not so much 'achievement' as 'space'. 'Making space for God in order to receive.'[3] That this is John's view of the Christian task may need some elaborating.

John uses two kinds of image in exploring our role. The first implies an earnest effort to attain. Climbing a mountain . . .

Just after his escape, before his busier years in Baeza and Granada, John spent a few months in the foothills of the Segura mountains. His ministry there involved a weekly journey of five or six miles over a hill to the sisters in Beas (the ones who had not been too sure about him when he first arrived). Retracing the journey, one can follow a meandering route which takes hours, leaving one hot and slightly irritated. There is, apparently, a more direct route. John would probably have made it his business to find this one, and take it.

To keep the sisters going while he was away, John wrote cards for each of them. One which he spread fairly widely (he made an estimated sixty copies) was a sketch of a mountain, with wide paths leading to dead ends, and one narrow path going direct to the summit. (Add the scrunch of sand and stones and we are with him on his route to Beas.) On the central path is the word '*nada*' – '*nothing*'. It is repeated all the way up – *nada, nada, nada, nada, nada, nada*, and on the broad, spacious, sunkissed summit, *nada*: 'Here there is no road, because for the just there is no law; she is her own law.'

The 'nothing' gets developed in the longer writings.

> To come to savour all
>     seek to find savour in nothing;
> to come to possess all,
>     seek possession in nothing;
> to come to be all,
>     seek in all to be nothing . . .
> to come to what you know not
>     you must go by a way where you know not . . .
> to come to what you are not
>     you must go by a way where you are not.[4]

This then is one image for 'progress': ascent. The image is demanding, radical, all-embracing. Here we come close to the gospel Jesus who asks for everything and evidently believes he is worth such a price. We come close too to the essence of loving, which, unless its dynamic is frustrated, will tend towards totality.

At the same time, it is important to understand the 'nothing' correctly. Here are some things it is not saying:

'Christian progress means forsaking whatever gives joy.' Of course not.

'Christian progress means striving for perfection.' Not quite this either, though John can use the word.

Apart from the fact that John intends to open a path to joy, and that his priority is not self-realisation (perfection), but relationship (union), a view of the journey from those perspectives would suggest that Christianity is one more test of excellence, which, in exalting the prima donna, tells the majority not to bother auditioning. If God is so far away, and it is so hard, better to let the demands of the gospel, and its promise, slip off into the shadows.

Trying again, 'Christian progress means: searching for the one who is giving joy to my life, who seems to believe in me, who makes me alive. When I am with him, every moment is a discovery; and being without him is like dying.'

This is, partly, what John is saying. That is why he writes, first, poetry, and why his poems relish the image of the lover's quest. Beloved – you wounded me – I went out – you were gone . . .

If progress is an ascent, then it is not the lonely labour of the athletic Christian. John steps out with vigour because the Other's love has 'wounded' him, and there can now be only one thing to care about.

Ascent; lover's quest, but both belong to one family of images, where the onus is on the person to take the steps towards encounter.

However, another kind of image is primary. We have seen it already in the symbol, 'flame'. In this case, it is the flame that does the entering; and the essential activity belongs, not to us, but to the Other, to 'the Spirit of her Bridegroom'.[5] In the *Living Flame* the entry is unimpeded and incandescent. Previously, as John portrays the journey, the approach felt more aggressive – like fire burning into wood, first making it sputter and steam, blacken and crackle, until the wood itself becomes flame.[6] But whether the flame is purifying or glorifying, it is the same 'fire of love' that is approaching, entering.[7]

This thrust keeps recurring: sunlight shining, eyes gazing, a mother feeding, water flowing, images of a God who initiates and invades. In this family of images, the emphasis is not on our forging a way, but on our getting out of the way. Progress will be measured, less by ground covered, more by the amount of room God is given to manoeuvre. 'Space', 'emptiness', are key words; or, as John puts it, *nada*.

This is what gets a person up the mountain. It has to be so. If John's writing springs from the impact of an invasive God, lavish in bestowing himself 'wherever he finds space',[8] the only meaningful asceticism would be the kind that clears the ground to make way for the onrush. All John has to say about our task must be interpreted in this light.

Writing to the Beas community, John speaks of people who 'do not stay empty, so that God might fill them with his ineffable delight; so they leave God just as they came – their hands were already full, and they could not take what God was giving. God save us from such unhappy burdens which keep us from such fair and wholesome freedom!'9

Hands empty and cupped to receive what God is giving: that does evidently depend on John's first word, a self-giving God. Otherwise, space just leaves you with space. *Nada* would be a sad word pronounced on its own. Instead, it is blessed because it always announces the presence of an 'everything' being given in exchange.

So it is that in John's sketch of the mountain, the summit is a huge space – 'and on the mountain nothing' – because it holds a total Presence: 'On this mountain dwells only the honour and glory of God.' A passage in the *Flame* catches the sense: as for God a thousand years are like a single day (Ps. 90(89):4) and 'all the nations are as nothing before him' (Isa. 40:17), so 'for the soul: all things are nothing to her. In her eyes, she herself is nothing. For her, only her God is everything.'10

This emptiness is gospel, not law; poetry, not prose. It is welcome to a God who is coming in to fill.

That is John's vision. It has an immediate consequence. The crucial question is not, What must I achieve?, but, What stands in his way? We shall look at that next.

# 7: Blockages

What can open us to an inflowing God? This is John's concern: not just to rearrange the pieces, but to make real contact possible. The *Ascent of Mount Carmel* is meant to address this. A word about that work first.

The *Ascent* divides into three books, showing just how unavailable we can be, then suggesting how we might cleave an opening. It is not the easiest work to read. It is methodical, and the author himself felt the weight of his method ('I know I often carry on too long . . .'[1]).

It is not the easiest to read; or rather, it is easy to read (the sentences are clear enough) but hard to read rightly; easy to think we have grasped it, when we have really grasped what we thought it would say, not what it did say. The author's contemporaries had the same problem: one of them says that John used to explain the work to them 'because it was so difficult to understand'.[2] Although the structure is obvious, its wisdom reveals itself only as one gets a sense of the whole: 'As you move further into it, the earlier parts will make more sense, as one thing sheds light on another.'[3] Read it twice, John ambitiously suggests.

If it is 'so difficult to understand', and life is short, we could be forgiven for wondering whether we should bother with it at all. Whether we read the book itself will depend on time and taste; but as to content, John has no doubt about its importance: it addresses the 'great need' of 'many people', offering a 'teaching of substance' which is 'good and very necessary'.[4] On offer here is something more than a rearrangement of the pieces: the author is proposing a way to break through the circle of our mediocrity.

So what does block God's entry? Where God is pressing in upon the person, the point of contention is her attitude rather than the things she has.

There can be a giving up of things which goes to extremes,

feeds the person's own ego and really amounts to 'the penance of beasts'.[5] For John, created beauty is beautiful – it has to be, if it is a reflection of the eyes of Christ. John's companions had no doubt about his appreciation, as he took them out into the hills around Granada, to let the fragrance of the mountains do what words and thoughts could only partly do. No doubt either about his esteem for art and form; it was obvious in his lush, visual poetry, crafted fine as filigree. In relationships, if there was any doubt, John was well able to dispel it: 'The last thing I want now is to forget you', he wrote to down-hearted Juana. 'Look, how could this be so with someone who is in my soul as you are?'[6]

John's love for his older brother Francisco is an instance of the value he set on friendship. Francisco's curriculum vitae was never impressive. With his wife, Ana, and the only one of their seven children to survive, Francisco remained poor. John loved to have him around. In a status-conscious society he would boast to visiting magnates, 'This is my brother – the greatest treasure I have in the world!'[7]

For John, created beauty is beautiful – people, art, nature. What concerns him is not so much the people or things being loved, as the loving heart. That is where freedom and slavery are played out.

> 'We are not talking here about giving up things, because that does not strip the soul if her affective drive remains set on them. We are talking about stripping away the craving for gratification (*gusto, apetito*) in those things. That is what leaves the person free and empty in their regard, even though she still owns them. Because it is not the things of this world that take up space in the person or do her harm. [. . .] No, it is the will and the hunger for them that dwells inside her.'[8]

The focus is on desire: if this gets out of place – 'disordered'[9] – it curls in on itself and chokes the person's openness to the other. Then the 'bonds of ownership' 'occupy the heart'.[10] At stake, then, is our ability to love; and the stakes are high:

> 'The person has only *one* will, and if this gets caught up in a particular thing, it will not be free, complete, single or pure – yet that is what is needed if God is to transform it.'[11]

When people, things, events are loved *within* God, there is harmony. When they get set alongside God – 'set in a balance with God'[12] – a process is begun in which affectivity groans under the violence it is inflicting on itself.

An extreme picture of this violence comes in the first book of *Ascent*. What at first is zestful and attractive – a role, a relationship, a project – then begins to make demands and has to feed on more of the same in order to sustain itself. It begins to claim the person's focus. Vision gets tunnelled, perspective gets lost, and one cannot see past what is now nose-close. Peace begins to go, and rationalising has to compensate ('it's quite normal'; 'it wouldn't be fair not to'). As the bonds become tighter, options must be made and good things are sacrificed ('I'll get all that sorted out at some stage') . . . until the final sacrifice of the person's self-worth. One is left with the aching awareness that this is all wrong, but that the possibility of changing it was renounced long ago. This is called slavery.[13]

John summarises the links in the chain: when desire is out of order, it increasingly causes fatigue, anxiety, confusion, a sense of guilt, and finally an inability to do anything about it.[14] It is a picture of addiction where the person's dependence is killing him. To put it mildly:

The group started well. They were enthusiastic, and I was keen to help. I sometimes felt I should let them try to get on without me, but that would not have been fair. They need me; and anyway, it really relaxed me being there. In fact, it was when I got home that I started becoming irritated, and it could take another evening with them to revitalise me. Now a couple of us have begun meeting informally two or three times during the week – I am convinced that the more we get to know each other, the better we will work together.

The only problem is, well, it's my wife. She seems to resent what I'm doing. Why does she have to turn it into an issue? I do have a right to my own space don't I? Anyway, if I carry on a bit longer, I'm sure the pace will ease off – the main thing now is not to spoil the balance we are getting in the group; it would be letting them down . . .

Disorder here, while it may bring gratification, ultimately kills joy. It is like the relationship which to begin with is healthy and life-giving; but if possessiveness is allowed to take over, anxieties creep in ('What will she think?', 'Should I apologise?'), situations have to be engineered, the 'relationship' ousts other values, and life revolves around it in tighter and tighter circles. 'Their concerns deprive them of all vitality, eaten up with care and a whole lot of misery. They do not allow joy to enter their lives.'[15] This, compared with the freedom of a love which does not have glue on its hands: it brings 'more joy, more refreshment'; 'this joy just cannot happen in a person who is possessively caught up.'[16]

If desires, not objects, are the crucial issue, the same malaise can occur with the holiest things. There is an infection in people who neglect their children, whether for their sport or for their prayer group. There is disorder in the person who has to have the last word, be it in the office or in the religious community. There is something not quite right when we need to feel emotionally high all the time, whether the feelings are coming from parties or from religion. Dependence: it may be on fashion, on status, on being needed, on feeling secure, or on a sense of spiritual well-being. John is seeking a radical cure, and a surface change is not enough.[17]

The point is that inwardly-centred desire closes up the space for communion between persons. That is when others turn into idols or into threats. To continue the earlier scenario:

> On top of all that there is this person in the group who seems to fancy himself as some kind of leader. At least, some people tell me I should give him a go at running it one evening. They do not seem to realise that the whole project is finely poised, and if somebody comes in full of bright ideas they could wreck in one night what it has taken months to build up. Things were going so well till he started nosing in. I'd better tell him to back off, or get out.

We become as big or as small as the objects of our love.[18] When the horizon out of which I am living is God, there is room to breathe. When it is less than God, the world becomes suffocating.

There is an alternative, and by this stage John's reader is meant to be saying, Yes – just tell me!

His answer comes to this: establish your freedom, by saying, 'no'. No, I don't need this. I need You.

I don't need it, not because it is bad, but because it is bad at the centre, and I want You at the centre. So today, on this occasion, I say, No. I don't need to write this letter or to make that phone call, today. I don't need to watch that programme today. I do not have to seek this person's affirmation, or to tell that one who is in charge. I do not need to do these things, not because they are necessarily wrong, but because I need You, and when I have shown myself that it is You I really want, then I can return to these others free, not as a slave.

John calls this 'denial': setting oneself free by saying 'no'. It is denying, not the thing or the person, but one's dependence on the thing or the person, so clearing a space for genuine communion.

Say 'no' where? At the point where my desire is most implicated, where I am not prepared to negotiate. Going beyond myself there will open a space, while heroism in other areas may really achieve little. In those other areas, I am already free. But it is here – this area of control, or pleasure, or achievement, or affection – that I am tied down, and a choice for God would give me wings.[19]

John says that a bird held by a thread is as 'held' as a bird held by a rope. The thread is easier to snap, but until it is snapped, there is still no flying. That seems to mean that, wherever desire is out of order, and we want it that way, and it is not a one-off but a habitual condition, then the situation has to be addressed.[20]

Here John is not being a perfectionist. He is not saying that every little last bit has to be tidied up. His God is a God of vast horizons, not of minutiae. John is not a perfectionist, but an extremist. His is the extremism of love, which 'takes off' when it is total. *Nada* signifies 'unconditional'; not 'unconditional except for . . .' If love is the driving force, there cannot be any area of life about which I say, Yes, but this area is not up for discussion. If there is such an area, love is liable to bring it on to the table.

That is the issue: affirming a greater love, and transcending one's cravings for the sake of that love. There are examples in John's writings of what might need transcending: the tendency to gossip;[21] the 'fears which make one faint-hearted';[22] a childish need to be propped up by others' approval;[23] the selectivity which makes one all available to the attractive person, but distant from the gauche or the smelly.[24] There are so many ways to stay small-minded. But whichever area of life may be one's battleground, the quality of one's whole life is involved. John, borrowing St Paul's vocabulary, speaks of two 'qualities' or levels: the level of 'sense' and the level of 'spirit'. It is worth pausing over this.

Tourism is great. It can freshen a person up marvellously. New surroundings, a different climate, local food; and the people! Most of all the freedom – there is perfect liberty to taste, to try, to meet, and to pass on, and so return to one's normal routine revived.

Tourism is great for a break. But it is a sad way of life. It means never unpacking one's suitcase, so never knowing the meaning of 'home'. It means plenty of acquaintances, but no deep friendship; a million sensations, but no inner growth; at best, there is the nostalgic ache for what might have been if I could have stayed longer.

The trouble is that there is a mesmeric fascination in keeping moving – there is nowhere so urgent as an airport. A fascination in moving, and growing fear of having to stop. It takes courage to 'stay with it': not to move on when I do not like it any more, but instead, to stay with it and let what is no longer novel disclose its unsuspected depth.

> 'Say 'no' to your desires, and you will discover what your heart really desires. What makes you think your longings are God's longings?'[25]

To live on likes and dislikes – *gusto, apetito*, gratification, affective drive – keeps one a tourist, doing more and more, experiencing less and less. This is to live on the level of 'sense'. It refers not so much to the sensory – the body, the emotions – as to the person who is hostage to his or her own needs. And the sensory side of the person can symbolise that: body and emotions are a rich blessing when they are in place, but they tend to turn imperialist and extend dominion over the whole person, making us 'sensual'. 'Sensual man': the person enslaved to each next moment.

If, however, a person chooses not to fill the hole with one more sensation, not to flit to another relationship or a different project, but to see this one through, life can transfer on to a new level. John calls it 'spirit'.

At first it can feel like starving. John tells of a 'language', 'taste', 'texture', a 'freedom', 'peace', 'life' which is yet to be discovered, and which we cannot know till it is discovered. 'To come to what you know not, you must go by a way where you know not.'[26] Not filling the gap with another novelty can feel like starving, but it allows the genuinely new to be disclosed. It allows one to live, not as a consumer among objects, but as a person among persons

– fit for communion, for the love which can hold the other, and be held, on open palms.

That is the level of spirit: availability as a person for communion; the space for the gift of the Other. This is more than just a rearrangement of the pieces.

# 8: Some Kind of Remedy

'No, I don't need this; I need You.' John puts it most sharply in his most misunderstood chapter. After his gruelling picture of the enslaved person, he proposes to offer, in chapter thirteen of the first book of *Ascent*, 'some kind of remedy';[1] some way of shifting from sense to spirit. It is meant to be helpful and realistic, but can seem disheartening and bizarre. It may be worth looking at the chapter more closely.

Essentially the message here runs: choose the person of Christ, and get used to making him, not your feelings, your ultimate basis for action. 'Not your feelings' – that is expressed clearly enough:

'And to bring peace to passion and lay it to rest . . . endeavour
   always to be inclined
 not to what is easier, but to what is harder . . .
 not to what is more, but to what is less . . .
 not to wanting something, but to wanting nothing . . .
 longing to enter in utter nakedness, and emptiness, and poverty,
   for Christ.'[2]

'Not to . . . but to . . .' The language is alarming, but three points should be made to set it in context.

First, there is an emphasis in the chapter on 'measure and discretion', on acting 'appropriately'.[3] Unless one wants to become unbearable quickly, it will often be 'appropriate' to do what is easier, and 'discreet' to choose rest. This ties in with the 'endeavour' ('endeavour always to be inclined to . . .'). It is John's word for meaningful effort and a wholesome pace. The author is not laying down in all this a crazy rule for blind obedience; he is making a serious point which it is worth trying to understand and apply in a realistic way.

Second, this is proposed as interim advice: it is not John's great contribution, but 'some kind of remedy', en route to inner freedom. While there will always be new thresholds, the freedom once achieved does not need to be constantly re-established. The person who has learned to swim does not need to keep learning to swim. The aim, John tells us, is to come 'very quickly' to a position of 'great delight and comfort'.[4]

So, third, John does not say, 'Always do what is harder . . .', but 'endeavour always to be inclined to . . .' That seems to mean two things: to see the value of, and to acquire the facility for.

To 'see the value of' being empty, less, poor. If the emptiness comes across as the lonely ascent of the self-made Christian, one is unlikely to be 'inclined'. If, on the other hand, we have heard John's word on the way God *is*: anticipating, enhancing, transforming, and pressing in to fill whatever space is given him – then emptiness will have an obvious value, and we will indeed be 'inclined' to it.

We shall also be inclined if we have ever experienced its opposite: the weariness of an over-demanding self-image, the claustrophobia of being 'full of oneself'; and the freshness that comes from being told that we do not have to be like that.

To 'acquire the facility for': that does not mean 'always do', but 'be able to do'. There will be challenges in life on which depend our growing as people. No one will blame us if we fail; it will just mean that we shall have missed the opportunity of becoming what we were always meant to be. The offer comes, and passes, and is gone, and we are still sitting, glued to ourselves. It would have been nice if we had responded, conscience told us to respond, but a rush of 'on-the-other-hands' crowded in to paralyse us. Such lack of inner freedom crippled Peter when the slave-girl started prying. It made Pilate panic when they began to mention Caesar. It keeps Christianity polite and well-meaning, but neutralises its power to change the world.

In order to remain supple for the moment of challenge that will one day come, get used, John says, to going beyond yourself. Make a point of not always doing just what comes most comfortably. Do not keep running, but do keep fit. This is 'acquiring the facility'.

If this is the programme in 1 *Ascent* 13, it is indeed far-reaching, but it is not bizarre.

So much for not living on one's impulses. There is more to the 'remedy', however. It begins with a 'yes', not a 'no':

48 *The Impact of God*

'First of all, have a constant longing (*apetito*) to imitate Christ in everything, so that your life takes on the form of his. And to do this, you must get to know his life, so as to be able to imitate him and respond in every situation as he would have done . . . Remain empty, out of love for Jesus Christ. He had no other gratification in this life, and sought none, than to do the will of his Father. He called that his food . . .'[5]

That is the meaning of the 'no': the affirmation of a greater love, 'a constant longing', for Christ. As fiancés would laugh if they were pitied for going out now only with each other, so for John there is something obvious about the streamlining that comes from having Christ at the centre. The choice for him begs a space for him, and gives meaning to the peeling away which life anyway involves.

Already life does involve plenty of streamlining. Staying with a dissatisfying commitment, being faithful to a difficult person, maintaining honesty in a dishonest climate, facing into a grey day – life almost forces us to go beyond ourselves. The question is, do we do so because we have no choice; or do we make it our choice? The demands of living, which borne mechanically may be just a series of suffered tragedies, can instead be 'yeses' to a greater love:

'And it is important in these matters to *put your heart into it*, and to try to align your will to want it, because if you work at it with the heart, very quickly you will come to find great delight and comfort . . .'[6]

This is John's vision of our task at its most practical: do what you do, but do it to please God.[7] We are being invited to look again at our activities, including their burdensome side, and to commit ourselves afresh to them each day, for God. It is simple; it transfers us to the level of spirit, and opens a space for the gift.

Saying 'no' to constant gratification, for the sake of a greater love; or saying 'yes' to the greater love, even when it costs: that is 'some kind of remedy' for our being closed in on ourselves. But there is a final point.

The 'no', and the 'yes', may come readily enough if this other greater love is a factor in one's life. But what if it is not? What if the real reason I am not stepping free from my enslavement, whatever it may be, is that I do not want to? Or that I only partly want to?

This is not a scenario on which John spends time. He takes for granted our sharing his conviction – for him the most obvious thing in the world – that God is an infinitely attractive proposition. As he writes in the white heat of the 'flame', we can hardly blame him for this. When he sings God's beauty in *Flame* and *Canticle*, he does so because he loves to praise God, not because he has to argue the case for God.

But the fact is that where John has no doubt, we may be less convinced; convinced perhaps in theory, but not where our desires are actually engaged. We may feel more like the young Augustine, who analyses brilliantly his own inability to step free, in his case from a lust which was holding him in 'hard bondage'. 'I almost made it, yet I did not quite make it.' He asks why his mind does not obey its own orders. His answer: 'it does not totally will; therefore it does not totally command.'[8]

Here the formula, 'Make space in order to receive', may evoke a limp 'I can't'.

However, to leave things there would be untrue to John of the Cross. His word was uttered first in weakness: he speaks under the impact of a God who searched out, came in, and created possibilities. His God is not more or less avuncular – good will and presents, but unlikely to overturn one's priorities. On the contrary, his gospel has eyes, powerful to create a fresh agenda and engage our life in their attractive power.

That is why, when John describes in *Ascent* our first steps on the Christian journey, he cannot help showing God to be the real protagonist. The person 'went out – *God bringing her out* – only out of love for him, *inflamed* in his love.'[9] She moves because 'inflamed' and 'brought'. Similarly in *Canticle*: the bride 'went out' because 'wounded' by Another. The whole enterprise is a response.

To step free from enslavement, we need a love which fills us at the point we thought the enslaving loves were filling us. To transcend our mediocrity, we need a love which touches us at the threshold of our fear. John presents a God whose love does that. Such is the conclusion to which 1 *Ascent* 13 leads: if our cravings and impulses are what normally inflame us, we need 'another greater inflaming by another better love, the love of [our] Bridegroom' – so, finding our 'fulfilment and strength' in this, we may have the strength 'easily' to stand free from any other.[10]

'Step free.' 'I can't!' Then try to let a different love set you free. Where love is concerned, there is no such thing as stalemate. The disaster would be, not our weakness, but isolation from this better love. The most useful thing to do is to admit this better love.

Practically, John advises, have the image of Christ around; acquire a 'passion' for him by 'getting to know his life'.[11] Let a new light into the situation by reading or thinking of the gospel Jesus. The gospel eyes shine through the gospel pages and can bring clarity in what seem impossible situations.

More practically still, let a new love into the equation. Have the person of Christ around, the risen Christ whose gaze is his love and whose love 'is never idle'.[12] Where other loves enslave us or our mediocrity imprisons us, there is a way forward: asking *him* to *give* us the love we are looking for elsewhere. 'Give me the love I am looking for in them.' That is the ultimate 'kind of remedy': to find a place where we can be with him and, for all our limp confusion, ask him, allow him, the 'principal lover',[13] to love.

This was John's approach, and, judging from a prayer of his, the source of hope in his own struggle.

'Who can free himself from his meanness and limitations,
if *you* do not lift him to yourself, my God, in purity of love?
How will a person
brought to birth and nurtured in a world of small horizons,
rise up to you Lord,
if *you* do not raise him by your hand which made him?
You will not take from me, my God,
what you once gave me
in your only Son, Jesus Christ,
in whom you gave me all I desire;
so I shall rejoice:
you will not delay, if I do not fail to hope.'[14]

# PART IV – Healing

## 9: 'Night'

> 'How will a person
> brought to birth and nurtured in a world of small horizons
> rise up to you Lord,
> if *you* do not raise him by your hand which made him?'

A self-lavishing God: that was the fact. From there came a word on our response: make space for the gift. Now comes the discovery: God undertakes to create that space. It is God who makes the 'space' – this for John is the real drama of our journey. He calls it 'night'.

Night: we cannot stop it, or hasten it; it just comes, and it teaches us every twenty-four hours that we are not in complete control.

John does seem to think there is something important here. Others speak of growth, suffering, purification, but 'we are calling' it 'night';[1] calling it '"dark night", very appropriately'.[2]

Up to this point John has shown himself a committed borrower. His ascetical demands are as old as the gospel text; and his sense of the 'givenness' of God is pure Easter (a risen Son spells a generous Father).

Where John stands out is in his following through the consequences of this when the temptation to interpret matters differently becomes overwhelming. When things turn acrid, contradictory, perplexing, back-to-front, when what should not be is – here John offers 'a serious word and teaching'; a discovery.[3]

This word is important today, in a world of swiftly shifting sand where foundations can be undermined suddenly. Life seems hopeful and purposeful; then circumstances conspire to break up the whole. A bout of illness coincides with humiliation at work; a friend seems not to care, or a relationship fails; my religion makes me feel more isolated, even foolish, especially after a chance conversation where principles I took for granted were questioned, even mocked. And prayer feels dead. All or some of these file away and together subvert the framework of faith out of which I was living my life. Life itself seems to have burst the hypothesis of God, and I can only collapse into some other hypothesis that promises to be, at least, more practical.

It is not only the events that are the problem. It is their suggestive power to destabilise: to undermine hope, or to cause panic. The negativity of life, its nightlike obscurity, does need, then, to be addressed.

John had a fascination for night-time which seems to have run in the family. His brother Francisco would sometimes be found outside in the fields late at night, lying beneath the starlit Castilian sky, arms stretched out in the form of a cross. So, long after dark, the friars would come across John outside near the trees praying, or he would be leaning at his window looking into the dark. It seems that he and his own were close enough to nature to let the natural world speak.

That is the first aspect of John's discovery: the symbolic quality of 'night', a symbol which speaks before ever we try to decode it. If John's primary word is his poetry, and his poems revolve around symbols, it is appropriate to soak in the symbol in its own right. The symbol 'flame' told us something about God; so the symbol 'night' tells us something about the journey. Our first step is, then, to let 'night' speak. Abstracting from any knowledge we may have of John's teaching, it is worth letting the resonances which night-time has for us surface.

Some words may come to mind: darkness, solitude, fear, the unknown, immobility, stillness, rest, peace, silence, sleep, dreams, moonlight, adventure, owls, stars, refreshment, friendship, romance, perception.

If these are the resonances, then such is the journey of faith. The 'night' symbol suggests, not organised gloom ('I think it's the dark night'), but that which comes upon us and is mystery, beauty, terror and new birth.

Part of John's genius as a poet lies in his ability to elaborate an image without choking its vitality. So turning now to his poem, *Dark night – noche oscura –* the 'discovery' retains its day-one freshness. As has been said, we may not feel at home with poetry. It may not appear 'applicable' to ourselves. But that is

not the point here, as we sound the soul of John of the Cross.
The point is rather that he, a pioneer in the Christian journey,
preferred to talk about it like this; when we ask him: 'Tell us your
faith story', this is what he wants to say.

> *En una noche oscura*
> So dark the night! At rest
> and hushed my house, I went with no one knowing
> upon a lover's quest
> – Ah the sheer grace! – so blest,
> my eager heart with love aflame and glowing.
>
> In darkness, hid from sight
> I went by secret ladder safe and sure
> – Ah grace of sheer delight! –
> so softly veiled by night,
> hushed now my house, in darkness and secure.
>
> Hidden in that glad night,
> regarding nothing as I stole away,
> no one to see my flight,
> no other guide or light
> save one that in my heart burned bright as day.
>
> Surer than noonday sun,
> guiding me from the start this radiant light
> led me to that dear One
> waiting for me, well-known,
> somewhere apart where no one came in sight.
>
> Dark of the night, my guide,
> fairer by far than dawn when stars grow dim!
> Night that has unified
> the Lover and the Bride,
> transforming the Beloved into him.
>
> There on my flowered breast
> that none but he might ever own or keep,
> he stayed, sinking to rest,
> and softly I caressed
> my Love while cedars gently fanned his sleep.

Breeze from the turret blew
ruffling his hair. Then with his tranquil hand
wounding my neck, I knew
nothing: my senses flew
at touch of peace too deep to understand.

> Forgetting all, my quest
> ended, I stayed lost to myself at last.
> All ceased: my face was pressed
> upon my Love, at rest,
> with all my cares among the lilies cast.

When John himself lets the symbol of night 'speak', that is what
it says to him. What resonances did he find? We could highlight
these: blessedness, and mystery.

Night, that which comes and curtails control, is greeted as a
'sheer grace!' – *¡Oh dichosa ventura!* – a night of beatitude. Its
darkness allowed a quest which responded at last to the demands
of loving, 'my eager heart with love aflame and glowing' (stanza 1).
It is the place for what is truest, deepest, most expectant: where
the light is within, surer than the noonday, fairer than the dawn
(stanzas 4 and 5). Most of all, John sees night as the place for
encounter – here, in the night; not after the night. 'Night that
has unified/the Lover and the Bride.' John's quest for union is
answered in this darkness, and it cannot but be 'blessed'.

But it is blessedness in mystery – nothing tacky or predictable.
John hangs the verses in suspense: long vowels and whispered
repetition, a hushed escape, furtive, three stanzas announcing an
open-ended search . . . Definition glimmers in stanza four: it is a
search for the other – but mentioned obliquely, 'one whom I knew
well'. It is a journey, precisely, at night. The blessedness is that
of Yahweh, whose angel passes between the two evenings, who
creates what was 'never heard, never known', and whose glory he
will not yield to another (Isa. 48:8, 11).

Having said that, John found these features had for him a distinct
flavour. He seems to have composed the stanzas, lush with their
Song of Songs imagery, in the peaceful months after his escape
from Toledo; but they come charged with what he learned there.

Hour upon hour of interminable blindness, blackness, in a stuffy
hole intended as a visitors' toilet. The midday ray of light

that poked through a slit high up in the wall served mainly
to mock the prisoner, as it passed on and pushed him back
into twenty-three more hours of heartless obscurity . . .

A person who has been through that and says 'dark night' means
something others cannot mean.

A change of gaoler brought a slight improvement: John could
empty his bucket once a day in the adjoining room – a glance
from the window, a crackle of mental notes and calculations,
then back to his dungeon. In the darkness, an option is forming.
It has John patiently loosening the screws on the lock, slightly, a
bit more each day; precisely measuring the length of his bedding,
to form strips that will reach from window to parapet; firming
up his will as his body keeps weakening. No place now for
indecision. Evening, night, eleven, twelve, one, two, half past
two. A single push on the loosened lock – 'God bless us!' says
a stirring friar. A minute, two, three . . . Silence again, and
bone-bare feet tip-toe between the sleeping guests to a window
that might just mean freedom.

A person who has been through that can say, in a way no one else
can, 'So dark the night, at rest and hushed my house, I went with
no one knowing . . . Ah the sheer grace!'
  John's Toledo imprisonment and escape gave to the symbol
'night' its full weight. In his commentaries the symbol is able to
carry humanity's pain, able to hold even such a sense of alienation
from God that the inner self feels dismantled – 'like one who is
imprisoned in a dark dungeon, bound hand and foot, unable to
move or see or feel any favour from heaven or earth'.[4]
  It is able also to hold the 'spiritual resurrection' which Toledo
had brought him,[5] the 'night that has unified . . .' The poem echoes
closely the 'Exsultet' song which the Church sings on Easter night,
where the paschal candle pierces the darkness as a sign of the rising
Christ. The Exsultet heralds Easter night as the union of heaven
and earth, the night of escape from Egypt, the most 'blessed of all
nights', chosen by God 'to see Christ rising from the dead!'[6] Night
carries all the weight of the Lord's passover.
  That is the resonance of the symbol for John. Night signifies
that which comes upon us and takes us out of our own control;
it announces that as the place of resurrection. A God who heals

in darkness – this is John's word of hope in a destabilised world.

It is important not to let the vitality of the symbol die as, in the following chapters, we enter into this healing darkness.

After John escaped from prison, he reached the sisters in Beas. It is said that, seeing him still fragile and subdued, they tried to raise his spirits with a song.[7] They chose a predictable little piece about love and suffering. John motioned to them to stop. He was trembling, weeping. He stayed there, clinging to a support, silent, for an hour. They allowed him to do that, even though no one understood it – how could they?

John's works rest on that silence. His symbols suffer if we try too hard to decode them. 'Mysteries' then become mere 'things' – if too specific, then exclusive, and thus irrelevant to the many. This can happen with two phrases characteristic of John: 'contemplation' and 'dark night'. Both speak of development in a person's relationship with God, particularly in prayer. They can sound abstruse. But in fact they convey mystery. They are really names for letting God be who he is.

Contemplation: prayer where I am no longer a tourist, where sense has shifted to spirit – where plenty of insights and aspirations have given way to a less picturesque, more total form of togetherness with God.

> 'Contemplation is nothing but a hidden, peaceful, loving inflow of God. If it is given room, it will inflame the spirit with love.'[8]

If God *is* a self-bestowing God, then his gift is liable to engage us. If he is active, then, in prayer, provided we stay around, he is liable to act.

Night: if God is beyond us, his approach is also liable to leave us feeling out of our depth. When the divine engages us more deeply, our minds and feelings will have less to take hold of, accustomed as they are to controlling the agenda, to meeting God on their terms and in portions they can handle. A deeper gift will *feel* like no gift at all. His 'loving inflow' is 'hidden'; it is night.

If anything is felt it will probably be our own selfishness and narrowness (wood crackling and twisting as the fire makes progress). When God approaches as who he is, I am liable to feel myself for what I am. As a physical sign of growth is growing pains, so a sign of God's gift is the pain of being widened. This is the blessedness of night, that God, who wants to give, undertakes to make space in us for his gift.

That, then, is the terminology: contemplation: a loving inflow of God; night: his love felt as pain.

Insofar as John uses these terms to describe a new phase in prayer, what he says will speak to some and not to others. Not everyone, in reading his commentaries on *Night*, will be able to say, 'Yes, that is what happens to me when I pray.' But in highlighting this phase, John is tapping into the way God is across the whole journey: God *is* a self-communicating God; and his gift changes people. The phase (contemplation, night) is symptomatic of a post-resurrection world.

So global statements are being made. Night assures us: that there is somewhere to go; that only God can take us there; that he does intend to take us there; that he takes us there in darkness; and that darkness must be lived in faith.

These statements will give content to the chapters which follow. But already 'night' has pinned John's colours to the mast. One might be tempted to consign him to a spiritual élite who have time for 'that sort of thing', and to get on instead with the ordinary business of Christian living. But what of those for whom ordinary patterns do not function, and who cannot 'get on' at all? In choosing 'night' – which comes down, comes upon, wrests control – as his symbol for the place where God loves to act, John offers a spirituality which embraces those who cannot get on. The disempowered, the inarticulate, and the pushed-around, are – if John's insight into God is true – a focus of God's action in the world. Here he is like the gospel Jesus, welcoming home those who were in the wrong place even to begin. John is standing by that: God's freedom, and the closeness of Jesus to the poor and the broken.

Night is taking us, then, not to some soirée for a self-preoccupied élite, but to the heart of the world's suffering. It declares the world's wounds to be spaces through which God may graciously enter. John's poem touches a universal chord; it is the song of the poor Jesus on Easter morning.

> This is the night when Jesus Christ
>   broke the chains of death
>   and rose triumphant from the grave . . .
>
> The power of this holy night
>   dispels all evil, washes guilt away,

restores lost innocence, brings mourners joy;
it casts out hatred, brings us peace, and humbles earthly pride.

Night truly blessed when heaven is wedded to earth
and man is reconciled with God!

(Easter 'Exsultet'⁹)

# 10: There is Somewhere to go

'One dark night . . . I went out.' That is the first thing John is proposing: a purpose. Time can seem to stagnate ('Nothing ever happens to me'), or to rush past uncontrollably ('I haven't a minute to think'). But whether it feels aimless or chaotic, John encourages us to interpret it as a journey, with a goal.

One of his models is the people of Israel leaving Egypt. At one level they were victims of the desert, caught in the land (cf. Exod. 14:3). The Bible, while acknowledging the hopeless zigzagging, yet reads it as a pilgrimage guided by Yahweh. Night means that: time does not just meander. It is a journey, to the Father.

The commentaries, *Ascent* and *Night*, tell us the same thing. John inherited a scholastic philosophy which thrived on subdivisions, but his basic analysis of the human person is simple. We have seen it already: humanity is sense, and spirit.

Sense means body, imagination, emotion. Spirit: there where resources converge, the home of choice, conscience, self. These terms are dynamic. When sense is lord, the whole being is 'sensual', hostage to needs of its own creation. If the person learns to live from within, she becomes 'spiritual', and, with that, her sensuality comes back home. All this implies a journey: a surrender of sense to spirit, and of spirit to Holy Spirit. And because surrender feels like dying, John calls it a 'night' journey.

As well as sense and spirit, John distinguishes between active and passive, what we do, and what is done to us. This yields a rather stocky four-fold pattern: active night of sense; passive night of sense; active night of spirit; passive night of spirit.

This can seem too technical to be true, and John warns against reading rigidity into it. For one thing, our effort and God's action run in tandem from the start. For another, our emotional life is really set in order only when our inmost self is purified.[1]

Still, the sense-then-spirit terminology is making an important point. It says that there is order and growth. Evidently, if life consists in sleep between orgies, then that needs addressing before spirituality will get much chance. But more broadly, the whole picture is one of progression. It confirms that Christianity is not just maintenance, but transformation. Our anthropology today may indeed be more nuanced. But whatever anthropology we use, John is saying that *every* dimension of the human person has to strive towards God, and, discovering the inadequacy of its striving, must come under his transforming hand.

This is already encouraging. John lived in an exploratory age. He calls his God 'rare islands',[2] and boyhood rumours of returning mariners surely lie behind the phrase. About the time he was beginning to write, the 'English pirate' Drake was raking Spanish holdings up the west side of the Americas, claimed some ninety years before by Columbus. As Columbus had sailed into the unknown, it is said that his fearful crew were on the verge of mutiny – mutiny, rather than come to the edge of . . . whatever. Columbus, in this perilous atmosphere, made a stark entry each day in his logbook: 'Sailed on'.[3]

John shows the same spirit of discovery, as one who has a purpose, and so can 'sail on' where others might grow mutinous. His journey leads within, to a love open to seemingly limitless increase.[4] He proposes relationship with Christ as *the* adventure – ¡oh dichosa ventura! – and, for him, the negativity of life was part of that adventure.

The journey has to feel like night because it leads into the unknown.

> 'It is like a traveller going to new lands of which he has no personal knowledge: the roads he travels are new – no personal knowledge of them either – and he will rely, not on what he knew up to then, but on what others say. It will be a journey in uncertainty.'[5]

If Christianity meant mere maintenance, then bewilderment or darkness would spell disaster. But if there really is somewhere to go, then darkness, the flip-side of the unfamiliar, is a condition of Christian life.

'Setting out on the path means renouncing your own path.'[6] Practically, one may have to renounce the satisfaction of seeing growth at the time of growth. It may be months or years down the track that one realises that a crippling weakness (say self-consciousness or fear) is no longer such a problem, èven though one did not see it disappearing at the time. What may have been felt at the time is a heightened sense of one's weakness – as wind feels stronger the harder we are pushing against it; a sense of our weakness, and an anxiety to be free.

Growth may not be felt at the time because what John holds out to us are not new ingredients, but a mellowing and maturing of what is most truly ours. He likens us to wine. People recently committed are like new wine: fresh, fizzy, and liable to go off. Mature love is like mature wine: no new bits, the same ingredients; but the batch will last, and the texture is smooth.[7]

Again, growth may not be felt because we grow in spirals, not straight lines. The same phenomena – darkness, restlessness, or inner peace – recur at different depths as John traces the journey. 'I'm the same as I was twenty years ago.' Maybe not: one may have spiralled deeper, though the scenery remains the same.

'To come to what you know not, you must go by a way where you know not.'[8] Growth may not feel like growth, and we need the encouragement that there is somewhere to go, if we are to 'sail on'.

What redeems the obscurity is the security of the guide: 'one that in my heart burned bright as day' (stanza three).

John holds spiritual direction in high regard: put simply, it is easier to get up when there is someone walking with you.[9] But he has little time for directors who force people into boxes. Each person's journey is individual, and no director has a map for all.

However, what makes him say this is not just regard for human freedom in an Inquisitorial, conformist society. He says it because he is convinced that there *is* a guide involved in every person's journey, whose leading other directors must not obstruct.

'Those who guide souls should realise that the principal agent and guide and motive force in this matter is not them, but *the Holy Spirit, who never fails in his care* for people; they are only instruments to guide people to perfection by faith and the law of God, according to the spirit *that God is giving* to the individual person.'[10]

John's ministry, like his life, depended on belief in God's involvement. This enabled him, as a pastor, to be earnest, but also to relax.

'Faith and the law of God . . .': he would direct people to where he believed the Spirit breathed freely – the word of Scripture and of his community, the Church – and then know that he was not indispensable.[11]

This implies a whole way of approaching ministry. Evangelisation here is not merely our task, entrusted to us by a now retired or exhausted Saviour. It continues to be his task; and his followers, sometimes, help. If in some instance they cannot help ('I don't understand what is happening to this person'), that need not be a disaster; the Spirit is the 'principal guide'. What is important is that his helpers at least do not get in the way. John's text continues:

> 'So the director's whole concern should be to see whether he can recognise where *God is carrying them* and if he cannot, leave them alone and do not disturb them.'[12]

Mission, like growth, is a journey into darkness. It rests on trust; trust that while at times we may not see a way, the Holy Spirit has a way, and will not 'fail in his care'. We shall return to this trust later. It is like viewing a tapestry from behind – a mess of threads. Only the principal weaver has access to the whole pattern it is making. Night demands we rely on his dexterity.

Those are two aspects of the night exodus: there is somewhere to go; and while the maps may be incomplete, the principal guide is infallible. Third, John tells us, the beyond is worth reaching. His witness to the impact of God comes from that beyond (the *Flame*). In *Night* he shows the beyond breaking in like dawn along the route. We shall look at some of its fruits: it means real growth in areas which it seemed would never change.

Night is, first, a journey into truth. It holds out the prospect of change to the otherwise ubiquitous ego.[13] The failure of our resources, submergence under what is too much for us, can enable us at last to stand in our truth before another. Where the other is God, this gets the name 'humility'. It means no longer being slave of a too-demanding self-image; knowing, not because we have been told it, or read it, or tried to convince ourselves of it, but because we *know* it, knowing that of ourselves we are nothing.

That is freedom. Job came to this after thirty-seven chapters wheezing under the weight of his own importance. Finally God answered: all he did was, kindly and very slightly, draw back the veil on who he, God, is. After that Job has little to say. 'I had heard of thee by the hearing of the ear, but now my eye sees thee; therefore I despise myself, and repent in dust and ashes' (Job 42:5–6).[14]

This is the freedom of being able to stand at the back of the temple and say, because now any other statement would be an irrelevance, 'God, be merciful to me a sinner' (Luke 18:14).[15] It means, not cringing submission, but the knowledge that I am part of something bigger than I had ever realised. It brings that mixture of awe, excitement and shame I feel when the one I had been instructing turns out to be a genius. It is knowledge of God which, John says, leads one to treat him with new 'respect' and 'courtesy'.[16]

With that comes the prospect of fresh sensitivity to other people's pain. Night softens the 'brittleness' towards others which comes from being full of ourselves.[17] When we know ourselves as we are, we can be mellow; 'gentle', John says, towards God, towards ourselves, and towards others.

> 'So the person no longer gets annoyed and upset at herself because of her faults, nor at her neighbour because of his, nor will she be displeased at God and disrespectfully quarrelsome for not making her good at once!'[18]

Relationships become simple. Where relationships may have been tangled ('Should I really be seeing this person?'), John promises us fresh air: 'When the person enters the dark night, night puts all these loves in order.'[19]

Night holds out the prospect, then, of standing in one's truth, of discovering the other's truth and, above all, of being released by that truth for love.

'You shall love the Lord your God with all your heart, and with all your soul, and with all your might' (Deut. 6:5–6). The ancient command continues to ring through Jewish and Christian liturgy today. The trouble is that it is impossible. We do not possess all our heart, all our soul or all our strength, for us to be able to love with them. The experience of the mystics confirms that there are depths of the human spirit which lie largely untapped.

What the night journey does – where that which comes upon us takes us out of our control – is retrieve our scattered human potential, place it in our hands, and so enable us, at last, to employ it in loving. This releases immense power. It may in part account for

the extraordinary effectiveness of Jesus and of some holy people.
From John it draws a unique statement of the greatness of all that
is human:

> '[Through the night], God gathers together all the strength
> the possibilities and longings of the soul . . . so that this total
> harmony can commit its strength and power to this love. In this
> way, she will come to fulfil truly the first commandment, which
> says – *rejecting nothing that is human* and excluding nothing
> human from this love – You shall love your God with all your
> heart and with all your mind and with all your soul and with all
> your strength . . .'[20]

Love can be a surprise to the one loving as much as to the person
loved. 'I never knew I could love anyone that much.' John is one
who did come to know and who holds out that horizon to us.

So, night brings a knowledge of our truth which eases us off
our self-importance and releases us for total love. Ultimately, it
is bringing another person:

> 'In the midst of this darkness and pain where love is present, the
> soul feels a certain *companionship* and inner strength, which
> accompanies her . . .'[21]

This helped us to understand John's experience in prison:
emptiness, the place of visitation. He speaks of a friendship
with Christ, increasingly sustaining, pervasive as light, but too
subtle to be seized.

Glancing at a clear night sky, thousands of starlets are faintly
glimmering. If we fix our gaze on one, it may seem to disappear
– as the part of the eye used to focus functions only in light. A
faint glimmer at night shows up in a general glance, but disappears
when we fix on it. Many good things are like that: they come when
we are looking for something else. Peace comes, if we are looking
not to feel peaceful, but to work for justice. Community comes, if
what we want is, not to feel togetherness, but to serve. Consolation
comes, if we seek not to be consoled, but to be faithful. The risen
one comes when we allow ourselves to die. 'In the midst of this
darkness and pain where love is present, the soul feels a certain
companionship . . .'

John says, then, that a journey which takes us beyond ourselves

– into night – is worth it. It holds out the inestimable blessing of knowing the friendship of Christ.

One last point about night as a journey. In the summer of 1591 a major meeting in Madrid showed up serious differences of opinion in the Teresian reform. John seems to have regarded some policies of the central government as unfairly harsh, and he objected strongly. While much is unclear, the fact is that John came out of the meeting without effective voice in the central running of the reform. Instead, he was on course for the mission in Mexico, 'the Indies'. He asked for volunteers (significantly, 'friends') who would willingly go with him.

Some weeks later the volunteers' signatures had been collected; but John's own destination had changed. A letter of his to one of them ('The letter consoled me immensely') announces that John was embarking for 'other, better Indies', where the treasures are 'eternal', and was preparing his luggage for the voyage.[22] He died later that year.

John's entire work is tensed towards eternity, towards the 'other, better Indies'. As the friars at his bedside began the prayers for the dying, John checked them. 'That is not necessary: read me something from the Song of Songs.'[23] He was interpreting his death as a mystery of love. He had written of death like this: 'The rivers of love which have long been flowing in the soul swell, bank up, like seas of love, as they press to pour into the ocean.'[24] Eternity meant to him love set free. That is where night is leading.

To share this sense of direction is not to downplay the goodness of the here and now. The world, and humanity, are beautiful; the mission is now; and God is here today. But bridges are for crossing, not just for enjoying. The knowledge that the bridge does connect with the opposite shore is highly relevant for what we are doing on it now. Eternity keeps today's horizons open. 'The first thing a person wants to do when she arrives after a long journey is to set eyes on the one she especially loves.'[25] All the lines of the Christian enterprise converge towards the absolute encounter with the risen Christ.

Despite the radiance of his experience, John's sense of the incompleteness of anything short of eternity remains vivid. Indeed, the more radiant the writing, the more vivid his sense of the shortfall. If, after a decade away, we were planning a visit home next year, but heard that the flight had been postponed by one day, that news would be manageable. If we have already landed, and are in the plane on the tarmac while our loved ones wait inside the terminal, the announcement of an hour's delay feels unbearable.

So for John, the lit-up faith of the *Flame* only accentuates the tension:

> 'However united a person may be with God in this life, she will never rest still nor be satisfied till her glory appears – *especially* now that she has savoured the taste of that glory.'[26]

Whether faith feels like 'fiesta' or more like a dull headache, we, like John, are in process. The process receives its energy from the future. It is being carried forward by the Spirit, who is 'bringing' the universe – soul, body, creation, relationships – 'into' Christ. 'For in all the blessings that God works for a person – the earlier blessings, the later blessings, the greater and the lesser blessings – the motive behind them all is that he should lift the soul to life eternal.'[27] Since the resurrection, the world and history are passive to a vast, divine, hidden agenda, drawing us into 'the centre of the spirit of the perfect life in Christ'.[28] Night – in life, and death – is doing that. It announces that time does not just meander. It is a journey, with a goal.

# 11: It Has to be God

'I feel so selfish – there is so much rubbish inside me.' John's reply would probably not be, 'You mustn't think like that', or 'You have to learn to love yourself'. He would probably say, 'Yes, you are right; but God means to free you.' If night first tells us that there is somewhere to go, it also announces that we cannot get there on our own. Progress means recognising that we cannot heal ourselves.

It is almost a cliché; but to grasp it as real in our lives is difficult for us. John summons up all his resources as a psychologist to help us.

We have already seen him go to extremes, in his picture of the damage ingrown love can do. That came in *Ascent*,[1] his first commentary on the *Night* poem, where his advice was, 'step free; say no'. But he shows himself anxious to get on ('no need to delay'),[2] because his real interest is in the processes which *set* us free. This comes in the second commentary, *Night*, the 'passive' aspect of the journey. Here he goes to extremes again, but this time to convince us that we cannot do the job on our own.[3]

The games we play, even in religious settings, to protect and promote ourselves, differ from age to age. The sixteenth-century Hispanic setting, with its relish for spectacular piety and penance, is John's immediate focus. Today, the symptoms are different: perhaps a need to multiply projects and discussion, with a fear of stillness or silence; a craving to be understood, and dismay when one's feelings are not recognised; a demand to keep one's options open, reluctance to make commitments that close the door on alternatives. Whatever the symptom, John is targeting the fundamental malaise: a passage through life which leaves us, in our inner self, still curled up in the womb position. That deeper malaise seems perennial enough.

Centred on oneself: John's words about envy are a good example.

'Many of these people [freshly committed in their spiritual journey] tend to feel repugnance at the goodness they see in others; they feel a real pain that others are doing better than they are on this journey, and they cannot bear to see others praised. To learn of others' virtues makes them sad, and sometimes they just cannot cope with it and have to contradict those compliments as much as possible.'[4]

We cannot heal ourselves, at least not deeply. We thought we had put things in order, then a chance remark about someone – 'She's such a nice person, always smiling' – may draw from us a reaction we thought we had dealt with long ago – 'Well wouldn't you be if you had as little to do as she has!?'

Envy, anger, pride – it seems to come from nowhere.

John can write of 'an unspoken self-esteem and pride' in people, which they never really recognise because 'they may be sunk in it up to the eyebrows!'[5] These attitudes come so tightly wrapped round our sense of who we are, of our place in the world, that they can be as invisible to us as the eyes we see with.

It is not so much a matter of being at 'fault'. These are tendencies more than choices, and they need a deep healing rather than just behavioural improvements.

We are given the example of people who have had a strong emotional experience (in prayer, but equally in the enthusiasm of a new project or the togetherness of a new group). When the lift passes, they feel empty. 'This distaste makes them disgruntled in what they are doing, and the smallest things get on their nerves, and sometimes they are so unbearable that nobody can put up with them!'[6]

It is a common enough scenario: a clash of frayed emotions on the first evening home after a retreat, and the unhelpful observation, 'If that is what it does to you, I can't see why you bother going!' Nevertheless, the distaste itself, while we do not have to wallow in it, is not a reason for blame:

'If they do not let [the feeling of emptiness] take over, they are not to blame for that natural reaction: it is an imperfection that has to be purged in the dryness [. . .] of the dark night.'[7]

Faced with this inbuilt weakness, one solution is to try harder. This may indeed help, but, John suggests, it will not cure. Nobody escapes their shadow by running faster. To run faster is one more exercise of our own expertise; but where even our expertise is infected, healing has to come from elsewhere. It has to 'come', and we have to learn to look for it to come. The waiting is part of the healing.

So John pictures for us people who get angry with themselves, wanting 'to be saints in a day'.

'Many make great resolutions and plans, but as they are not humble, and have no distrust of themselves, the more resolutions they make, the further they fall, and the more annoyed they become. They do not have the patience to wait till God gives them what they seek when he so desires . . .'

Healing cannot be engineered; it must come, like night, and from God:

'This [frustration] runs counter to [. . .] gentleness of spirit, but it can only be completely remedied by the purgation of the dark night.'

And the author ends wittily:

'Some people, however, are *so* patient about their desire to go forward, that God would prefer to see them a little less so!'[8]

Leaving that last vignette aside, John is saying all this, not to be ironic ('Think you'll see some change in your life?!'), nor to be bleak ('Yes, the right idea, but you're nowhere near the standard'), but rather to bring us to an admission.

It is not surprising that the admission comes to us slowly: it took Israel most of her history to learn it. It came first mixed with blood and slaughter – 'the battle is the Lord's', said David to the Philistine. Filtered through defeat and exile, it came to be made more purely, praising the Lord 'who raises the poor'.[9] The admission is that, ultimately, and in my own case, salvation must come from God.

As with Israel, so for ourselves, the lesson may arrive wrapped in circumstances that seem over-exacting: family members cutting loose; a loved one whose addiction is destroying him; one's own nervous resistance suffering under excessive demands. And these circumstances do of course need addressing. But they can also be an occasion of surrender and discovery: surrender of my hold on the other person; discovery of a new level of resources. This can lead to the admission that, ultimately, I am not the one who saves. I am not my saviour; I am not her saviour. God is our saviour. One passage puts it uncompromisingly:

> It is fitting that the person do what she can, so that God will 'put her in that divine surgery, where she is healed of all of which she could not heal herself. For however much the soul might help herself, she cannot by her own effort purify herself so as to be disposed in the least part for the divine union of perfect love, if God does not take her hand.'[10]

Francis Thompson (poet, sometime opium addict, pursued by the 'Hound of Heaven') penned his own epitaph: 'Where I find nothing done by me, much may have been done in me.'[11] 'Night' is saying that. Healing comes from God.

That is one reason why healing must come from elsewhere: we are too bound to ourselves to be our own liberators. Another is that, even were we free, the ultimate healing lies beyond our grasp. The real 'wound' is our need for God, and God himself must be the cure. But God – especially John's God – cannot be conquered or achieved; he has to give, and must be received. In a scientific age which thrives on achievable goals, this lesson too comes slowly.

'Between Creator and creature no similarity can be expressed without including a greater dissimilarity.'[12] This rather sturdy sentence from the Fourth Lateran Council in 1215 has huge implications for the way in which we talk about God. Words do what words can: they point us in a direction. But in the case of a God whose otherness is total, description falls so far short of the goal that any 'like' has to be qualified with a greater 'unlike'.

So we say that God is powerful. We know what power is: it is there in the wind and the ocean; in horse-riding and fast driving. We know of powerful people. So we know power and say that God is powerful. 'Well . . . yes. But God is more unlike that power than like it.'

God is love. We try to love and others may have loved us. So we know what love is and we rightly say that God is that. 'Well, yes . . . but God's love is so much greater: the difference outstrips the resemblance.'

While knowledge and control are good, we are called to celebrate what we do not know, someone we cannot control. The mystics serve to remind us of this. Far from having fathomed the divine, they say, 'We do not know'. 'Of God himself', John writes, 'nothing could be said that would be like him.'[13]

Police sent to arrest Jesus return empty-handed. 'Why did you not bring him?' . . . 'No man ever spoke like this man!' (John 7:46) While the gospels say much about Jesus, they rejoice in what they cannot say. 'Something greater than the temple is here.' Greater than Jonah, greater than Solomon; and those who have met him are 'amazed' (Matt. 12:6, 41–2; Mark 10:32).

This is the Christ of St John of the Cross: an unfathomable mine, 'with seam after seam of treasures'.[14] This Christ is a window on to the unfathomable Father, whose approach leads John to say, 'We don't know.' It leads him to 'understand clearly that everything remains to be understood'.[15] This God is invitation, beauty, and permanent surprise. And heaven will not dissolve the mystery; it will set us free for it entirely. It is the saints and angels, John says, who find God 'always new and increasingly amazing'.[16]

John celebrates, then, the otherness of God. If God is so 'other', then his friendship has to be given, it cannot be conquered. A Christian must be one who waits 'till God give them what they seek when he so desire'.[17] There is somewhere to go, and it has to be God who takes us there.

# 12: Healing Darkness (I)

We said that night typically refers to a growth in prayer, but that this shows up wider realities. We have looked at two: that there is somewhere to go; and that only God can take us there. This brings us now to the heart of John's witness: that God does act to take us there – a God who transforms in darkness.

To be true to John, it should be said that not every suffering is night. But any suffering can become night. For it to be night, there have to be three elements. For it to be a 'sheer grace', in darkness, leading to union, there has to be:

– an inflow of God;
– darkness – that is, the suffering, with the accent on bewildering suffering;
– a creative response – faith, acceptance.

First, an inflow of God. The admission that we cannot heal ourselves, while it may take some tension out of the air, fails of itself to hold out hope. What makes 'night' blessed is the added assurance that the one who can heal does intend to heal. Where God finds space, he enters. This was John's first word: a God pressing in to bestow. That is what makes night something other than disastrous.

Except for the conversations his captors feigned at the door of his dungeon to break his morale, John heard few sounds in prison. One sound he could hear was the river Tajo which circled tongue-shaped round Toledo. The city wall in which John was closeted dropped down to this river below: water flowing, sometimes torrential, sometimes inaudible. It came to symbolise for him the flowing creativity of God – always torrential, but known in the inaudibility of faith. A fountain that flows by night. This formed the refrain in another of his prison poems.

> *Qué bien sé yo la fonte . . .*
> I know so well the fountain, rushing and flowing
>      though it be night.

The stanzas tell of an ocean-sized waterfall, which is Father surrendering to Son, Son self-emptying to Father, Spirit-water spilling out to create a universe; the cosmos comes to sip it, though all – heaven, people, hell – are already drenched in it. John knows it, believes it; and he sees it welcomed, cupped and offered to him in the Bread of Life:

> That everlasting fountain comes concealed
>      in this living bread, to *give us life*
>           though it be night.

This poem, '*La Fonte*', provides another avenue on to what was most precious to John at the time when all he valued was being desecrated. The verses transmit his experience, known in darkness – night, faith – of a God whose love is bursting its banks. In this poem, that love takes on the form both of Eucharist and of community – at the time when prison was depriving John of both.

John belonged to a movement, a religious order, which proclaimed salvation by community. Its Rule proposed a life in common as 'brothers'.[1] Yet companionable John knew bitterly how the brethren could fragment into acrid factions. He was in a dungeon in Toledo because of that. The thrust towards community, then as now, had a good chance of tailing off into cynicism.

This took John to the roots of his Christian faith and he found there grounds for not growing cynical. His hope lay in the fountain – Father surrendering to Son . . . There is a unity in the cosmos which comes from the Trinity. John asserts: Your thirst for community is not an illusion because it issues from God.

His '*Fonte*' sings of a God who *is* community. Father, Son, in Spirit: living water in infinite personal exchange. And that God is community with a *maximum* immigration policy. As close friends can together be deeply compassionate to others without feeling threatened (a married couple can welcome friends in a way fiancés cannot), so the Spirit-rapture of Father and Son lets them issue an entirely open invitation. Theirs is a love secure

enough to let them be vulnerable. So John knows a living
water which just loves to overflow so as to gather all else in
its flow.

In '*Fonte*' John shares his faith too in the Eucharist. For him,
Eucharist is not simply our ritual galvanising our togetherness. It
is an act of the Trinity involving us in their togetherness. Nor is
Eucharist a merely *passive* object of adoration. It is an activity of
Christ, powerfully 'summoning his creatures' to the water (stanza
twelve). John sees Christ here active, torrential, receiving the full
force of all that God is and unleashing its flow upon us – the
'everlasting fountain' released in the living bread 'to give us life'
(stanza eleven).

The 'Fountain' poem gives us, then, one more phrasing of John's
glad tiding: God *is* an inflowing God. This, for John, was practical
spirituality. It enabled him to survive. The same resource sustained
him in the final disgrace at the end of his life. Details of that are
worth relating here.

We mentioned John's opposition to new policies in his Teresian
Order (a decade after John's escape from Toledo, and some years
after Teresa's death). Though he reacted strongly where he saw
injustice, he was not impervious to the emotional strain.

He had confessed to Marina, a nun in Segovia, that before he
went to the meetings of the central council, he would spend time
in prayer, and, whatever ambiguity there might be on the floor,
he kept to the light which prayer had given him. The situation
deteriorated, and Marina asked him, 'Does your Reverence still
follow what God gives you in prayer?' Her account goes on, 'I
could see he was upset, and his eyes filled with tears. He couldn't
stop himself, and I said to him, "Things must be hard for you,
Father." He replied, ". . . I don't say anything any more, Sister
Marina, because they do not listen to me."'[2]

Once it was clear that John had lost influence in government,
enemies had a free hand. A campaign of libel was initiated against
him; compromising testimonies were extracted and distorted;
people were scandalised as John came closer to being thrown
out of the Order for which, years previously, he had nearly died.

Now, in 1591, death did intervene. While his body was suc-
cumbing to erysipelas, his heart and reputation were still being
battered. The prior of the community of Ubeda where he had
gone for treatment had a grudge against him, and made his dying

quite difficult. Medicines were regarded as a financial drain, putrid bandages were not to be washed, visits were curtailed . . . John's nurse, Bernardo, captures it with a modern phrase: 'It was just incredible what was taking place!'[3] Finally, Bernardo himself was forbidden to nurse John. Whatever about the sick man's patience, Bernardo had had enough: he wrote in complaint, higher authorities intervened and matters improved in time for John to die in a community at peace.

Through all this – the sidelining, the libel, the dying – John seems to have been drawing on a different source of energy. A letter written from Ubeda puts it this way:

'Love greatly those who speak against you and do not love you, because in this way love will come to birth in a heart that has none. That is what God does with us: *he loves us, that we might love him, through the love he has for us.*'[4]

That is the God to whom John bears witness: a God loving first, with a love which creates good in us; a God pressing in to release new capacities in us. This is his over-arching vision when he comes to speak of the night of suffering.

If the first requirement for night is an inflow of God, John is not saying, 'In certain experiences God gives himself, in others he withholds himself, and our interest is in the former, only.' It is true that the divine inflow may be resisted; true, too, that it may be experienced in different ways. But John's greatest contribution is not a distinction ('God has started flowing in if you see the following signs'); it is an assurance: 'God is *always* flowing in.' More important than the signs is the sunshine which makes any of the signs legible. As John puts it, if we play our part . . .

'It is impossible that God fail to play his part, by communicating *himself*, at least in a hidden way. It is more impossible for the sun not to shine in a tranquil, open place. The sun is up early and shining on your house, ready to shine in if you open the curtains. So God, who never sleeps nor slumbers as he keeps watch over Israel, will enter the empty soul and fill her with divine blessings. God is like the sun, shining over souls, ready to communicate himself to them . . .'[5]

An inflow of God: that is always at hand. It is not God's absence, but the *way* he is present, that may cause us difficulty. This brings us to the second ingredient: the darkness, or suffering which is, especially, bewildering.

# 13: Healing Darkness (II)

John of the Cross does not impose suffering. Robust though he was, he knew how damaging pain could be and showed himself attentive. It is said that, when he noticed one of his religious brothers looking unhappy, he would go out with him for a walk in the garden or the fields, and come back only when he had cheered the man up.[1] There seems to have been an extraordinary empathy between him and his own community. In Fray Martín's estimate, each of them 'loved him more than their own father'. He reports that whenever John returned to the monastery, 'those of us who saw him would all hurry out' to meet him, 'so great was the brothers' joy at seeing him return'.[2] There was in him none of that harshness which makes the exercise of authority straightforward, was a feature of his age, and which he qualified as a 'vice proper to barbarians'.[3]

When John speaks, then, of night, of that which comes upon us and wrests our control, he is not imposing suffering. Suffering is a fact, and John's intention is to encourage us to bear it creatively.

One conviction that John clearly has is that suffering is not foreign or alien to God. If the cosmos is drenched in the Fountain water, everything in it can be a channel for that water. If God's gaze holds the world in being, it holds it all in being, including its pain.

This led John to make startling statements in his letters, during those final months when others' behaviour was causing him real affliction. Not only did he seek to meet the enemy with the love God gave him; he also tried to see the enemy as bearing God's love to him:

'As for my situation, daughter, do not let this cause you pain . . . It is not men who are doing these things, but God, who knows what suits us best and orders all things to bring us blessing.

Think nothing but that God ordains it all, and where there is no love, put love, and you will draw love out.'[4]

'God ordains it all . . .' Surely not; at least not in the sense of wanting the pain as pain, or of working to create it.

In a Christian view, God respects the laws of nature, entrusts the world to human freedom, and works through secondary causes more than miracles. John is strong on this;[5] yet he, like most saints, seems to have seen even the details of his life as the will of God for him.

Both 'natural laws', and 'divine providence': this is one of the Christian both/ands which we may never manage to explain, but which come to make sense as one strives to live in faith. In the case of brutal suffering, it is 'both' awful, inadmissible, often the result of others' sin, something to be remedied, in danger of turning us in on ourselves; 'and' it is held in God's love and can be said to be God's will for me now.

So, short-cutting, and taking a whole lot for granted, but making what he considers a vital point, John encourages us to see a God-content in the negativity of life. He encourages us to view 'all the struggles and difficulties' of life as 'coming from the hand of God, for the person's good. This is the remedy. She should not run away from it, because it is healing for her' and brings a 'great blessing'.[6] That comes in the *Flame*, where John is asking what can release a person for the impact of God. The message comes in a more homely way in one of his sayings:

'When you are burdened, you are joined to God. He is your strength, and he is with people who suffer. When there is no burden, you are just with yourself, your own weakness. It is in the difficulties which test our patience that the virtue and strength of the soul is increased and affirmed.'[7]

'Night' presents suffering, not as the only place, but as a privileged place of God's inflow. In it, love not only comes; love also opens a space for its coming. That is the God-content of pain: it has power to unlock us at the point we cannot unlock ourselves. This accounts, though, for a second conviction: that healing comes particularly in situations that take us out of our own control, in the kind of pain which is bewildering. We shall follow John as he uses the tenderest of images to convey this: that of a child being nurtured by its mother.

In John's ministry, work with children did not figure highly – although children do seem to have felt at home with him, judging from the way the street kids in Avila warmed to the young chaplain.

The nearest John came to a more long-standing commitment was when he was accosted in Granada by a woman carrying a little boy. She asked him for money to feed him, because, she said, John was the father! The nonplussed friar tried to ignore the lady, but as she insisted, he asked who the mother was. 'A young noblewoman.' 'Where is she from?' The mother, it turned out, had always lived there in Granada. 'And how old is the child?' 'Just over a year.' 'Now that *is* a miracle: I've been in these parts for less than twelve months!' John apparently got extensive mileage from the episode when he wanted to make people laugh.[8]

Whatever about children, John did have plenty of close-hand experience of a mother's difficulties. We saw that, while John was still a baby, his mother Catalina, like many victims of mid-century famine, had to traipse around Castile in search of better conditions. Twelve-year-old Francisco would walk beside her, while she carried John on her back or in her arms. Later, when John was six and nine, they were on the move again (Arévalo, Medina del Campo): no carrying this time; all three had to walk.

There was occasional income. Along with her weaving, Catalina made some money as a wet-nurse. Señor Velásquez de Mirueña quaintly maintained that he 'would give four *reales* a month more to Catalina Yepes than to any other, so that his daughter could be nursed by so virtuous a woman'![9]

Catalina nursing and weaning children; Catalina carrying her baby on long journeys. John uses both images: a mother weaning a child so that he might grow; a mother, picking up and carrying a child, so that he, and she, might actually get somewhere. For John, both images speak about God: they convey that God is constantly active, his love motherly and creative; and that this constancy will feel disconcerting, like non-milk food for a baby being weaned, like loss of contact with terra firma when mother whisks the toddler away.

The passages run like this: first, God as the mother weaning the child, enabling him to grow.

'When a person turns to the service of God with real determina-
tion, God normally nurtures his spirit and warms his heart, as a
loving mother does to her little child – she warms the child at the
breast and feeds him with sweet milk and mild and sweet food,
and carries him in her arms and hugs him. But as he grows, the
mother [. . .] puts him down and makes him walk on foot. She
does this so that he can leave behind childish ways and take on
greater things, more real things.

'It is the same with the soul: the *loving mother of the grace of
God* brings him to rebirth through a new warmth and enthusiasm
for serving God: [. . .] God offers him sweet and satisfying spiritual
milk, without effort on the soul's part, and great attraction for
spirituality . . .

'[But when] God senses that he has grown up a bit, God
draws him away from the sweet breast and puts him down
and gets him used to walking on foot so that he can grow
strong and leave his baby-clothes behind; and he finds this
new phase bewildering, since everything has turned back-to-
front.

'[Here] 'God gives the person to taste the food of the strong,
which in this dryness and darkness [. . .] the spirit begins to
receive in its dry emptiness.'[10]

That is one image: mother helping a child to grow up. So John
perceives this to be a sign of God's action in a person's life: their
relationship with God ceases to be liquid comfort, loses its feeling
of feed-back, perhaps of romanticism. Maybe the person had a
way of praying with the gospel, or of telling over the words of a
favourite song, or of picturing Jesus and expressing her feelings
to him. But the point comes where these no longer feed her, and
the only appropriate stance is attentive, loving stillness before one
who is greater.

To the person herself, this looks like loss of the only colour on
her religious horizon. It is bewildering – have I done something
wrong? why have I lost something so evidently life-giving?; and
here it is the fruit, John maintains, not of God's withdrawal, but
of his maternal love drawing closer.

The second image confirms this: the mother carrying the child,
doing for him what all the child's toddling could never do. The
frustrated infant may misinterpret the assistance, and register an
appropriate protest:

'It can happen that God is working to keep the person in that quiet stillness, and she is struggling with her imagination and thoughts, and wants to work for herself. It is like a little boy: when his mother wants to carry him in her arms, he starts screaming and fighting because he wants to walk; so he gets nowhere, and he holds up his mother!'[11]

Loving mother: an image of God's constant care; but also of the suffering that the journey into his love must involve. And the emphasis is not just on pain, but on the disconcerting: '. . . they find this new phase bewildering, since everything has turned back to front'.

When John wants to portray this reversal in its least diluted form, he talks about mystical prayer; prayer, then, where the divine approach is registering in the mind and feelings, but registering here as painful contrast. As human, the person is out of her depth; as sinner, she is suffering the contradiction between what she is and the atmosphere of love she is breathing. The whole scene is antagonistic.[12]

That is the mystical 'night', the darkness of God's immediacy. Yet, as John holds that all events are rooted in God, so any reversal can carry his approach. John's own night involved unjust imprisonment when he was thirty-five and a campaign of libel at forty-nine. In the case of others, he is able to apply night language to the most unmystical afflictions: financial difficulties; loneliness; being let down by friends; being misjudged by authorities; friction in community.[13] Depression too can have a part in it.[14]

Presumably we can add our own reversals to the list: unnecessary changes in what was held dear; repression where one had come to enjoy new freedom; the company of people who mock or side-line one's convictions; the difficulty of believing; the uncertainty of the future; the great reversals of bereavement, illness, ageing and dying – 'the trials that ordinarily and humanly happen to all who live'.[15] It is correct (with John Paul II here) to widen the scope:

'Physical, moral and spiritual suffering – like sickness, the plagues of hunger, war, injustice, solitude, the lack of meaning in life, the very fragility of human existence, the sorrowful knowledge of sin, the seeming absence of God – are for the believer all purifying experiences which might be called "night of faith."'[16]

Night is the right word: darkness, where vision no longer functions, and one has to fumble one's way along slowly, feeling for
the wall. To offer three scenarios:

> We have been working hard to educate our children; it means
> sacrifice. Sometimes too much sacrifice, with commuting to work,
> cut-backs in life-style, and the lack of space just to be together;
> there seems to be less and less fun. It is hard; but we want to
> do it. Then a letter comes, confidential and quite curt, from
> the headmaster. 'Our daughter has been caught in some heavy
> drugs-linked thieving; it looks serious'. . . This is night pain: it
> is 'bewildering, since everything has turned back to front'.

> It was coverage of the street children that finally made me
> wake up: 'there is a world out there, and I'm responsible'. With
> the encouragement and some help from the diocese, I gave up
> my job and went on a training course in poverty awareness. It
> was hard; I suppose I missed the prestige my work used to give.
> But I saw it through and now I am, well, nervous but ready . . .
> And the news comes that the diocese is no longer interested.
> Not just harder, but back to front.

> I do not want to go back on my decision. But I don't under-
> stand what is happening to me. My life had been hollow and I
> used to try to fill it with glossy relationships which just sounded
> tinny when you tapped them. When I fell in with a different
> group and started to pray, all the loose ends came together and
> there was purpose and energy, enough for a real change in my
> life. Since then I have spoken about my own journey to countless
> people, and it seemed to help them. But now I feel a fraud. I
> come to pray – a lot – and there is no more sense of presence.
> It doesn't hold my interest the way it did. It's not that there is
> some alternative; but the whole scenario has just flattened. I
> thought at first I was having an off-day (I know mood can affect
> prayer). But it was the same the next day, and the next; it has
> become a pattern. . . . Not just hard, but back to front.

This is the night, where there is not only pain, but where the ground
I stand on to face the pain seems to shift.

How far can the reversal go? It may cut deep. John speaks of a
'night of the spirit'. It may strike, then, at the level where I connect
as a person.

If it is true that our centre is not self, but God – 'the centre of the soul is God'[17] – that means that we become 'centred' by surrendering our 'selves' for the sake of this Other. That sounds fine, but in practice we cling to ourselves with all the life-force that is in us, and to be cleaved off ourselves means a dying. Burglary, or exam failure, or prostrating flu, are disturbing enough. But there exist treasures wrapped more tightly round our sense of who we are, and losing them is like being violated.

John gives examples of that sense of violation. A person who wants to live uprightly can be tortured by scrupulosity, where every action seems a potential sin. A person wishing to be holy in body as well as spirit can feel swamped by sexual phantasies. Someone wishing their faith to be central can find themselves victim to blasphemous thoughts.[18] This all deeply questions such people's security and cuts into the basis of meaning from which they live.

The questioning may reach through to the ultimate meaning, one's relationship with God. If the living God, and not our image of God, is to fill the emptiness of the human spirit, even that image – the closest thing we have got to God himself – may need dismantling. 'I am not what I thought I was. God is other than I thought God to be.'

John describes such peeling off of the spirit's skin as a sense of 'disintegration'.[19] He speaks of the 'greatest suffering', 'the anxious thought that she has lost God and the fear that she has been abandoned by him'.[20]

Here too John surely writes from his history. Perhaps in his Toledo prison the wounds up his back and the sense of failure in his reform project were uppermost in his mind; but more deeply undermining was the company of a silent God, whose company lit up John's unworthiness and whose silence could feel like rejection.

When John later had time to relate his experience, he perceived it as 'the loving mother of the grace of God', undoing him to recreate him. He became certain of this. He could even write poems about it. But at the time, in night itself, he felt he was brushing the borders of 'hell', and it seemed to him dark as chaos.[21]

One of John's most uncompromising disciples was Thérèse of Lisieux (1873–97). Thérèse Martin died slowly at twenty-four from tuberculosis. During the year and a half of illness, her sisters jotted down remarks of hers; the documents testify to her heroism and humour in a religious climate which could be decidedly clammy. Thérèse was able to face into it with a light touch because she lived with a larger horizon – the one to which her whole life had been directed – that of the fullness of love which she understood heaven to be. Yet in her final year, it was this, her hope in what lay beyond death, which was being undermined. She shared the experience with her religious superior. She said it was a 'dark tunnel'.

> 'And now all of a sudden, the mists around me have become denser than ever; they sink deep into my soul and wrap it round so that I can't recover the dear image of my native country any more – everything has disappeared.
>
> I get tired of the darkness all around me . . . I hear its mocking accents; "It's all a dream, this talk of a heavenly country, bathed in light, scented with delicious perfumes, and of a God who made it all, who is to be your possession for eternity! You really believe, do you, that the mist which hangs about you will clear away later on? All right, all right, go on longing for death! But death will make nonsense of your hopes; it will only mean a night darker than ever, the night of mere non-existence."'[22]

Thérèse feared having said too much, yet felt she had not said enough. Everything in her religious world had been subverted, bar the most naked believing.

What can one do to help a person going through the night? The presence of a friend can be a vital support. But there may be nothing useful to say. It can be that explanations bring worse isolation: 'I can't be getting it across, if that's how they see it.' 'They may be right, generally, but it doesn't apply in my case.' John envisages a person 'finding no consolation or support in any teaching or spiritual guide'[23] – a sense of fitting none of the patterns available. Even prayer may be reduced to a silent haemorrhage trickling into one's spirit. There seems to be a prayer of not being able to pray: where it is 'not the time to be talking to God', but to lay one's lips 'in the dust – there may yet be hope . . .'[24]

That is the focus of John of the Cross: a night that spells bewilderment; all the spokes of the wheel pointing inwards, and the hub taken out. John has taken us to those outer regions, which lie beyond the threshold of our own resources, the unfamiliar lands of birth and death; he is calling that the place, not of chaos, but of transformation.

Greater than the temple, greater than Jonah: God is greater than our feeling of God, greater than our concept of God. When our lights no longer offer support, when our sense of worth or place or progress is growing dim, when what should not be, is – then a God who is greater than we are has room to impinge.

If Christianity were a human enterprise before a spectator God, this would not be so. Darkness would mean only darkness. But if the enterprise is divine, and the divine is pressing in to fill, those outer regions can be places of healing. They offer the emptiness God needs to pour himself out entirely.

In writing *Night*, John does not want to say, 'It's all right, you see, because this is the explanation.' He wants to say, 'It's not all right; it's a mess. But you are not alone in this. God is present in this. Now is the time not to lose faith in him.'

That is the third element to night. An inflow of God, the suffering which bewilders, and the response – not to abandon faith in him.

# 14: Beyond Sympathy

Sympathy can be ruinous. 'I think it's dreadful – I don't know *how* you put up with it. No, I really can understand, you must feel *awful* . . .' Then, 'I'll pop round again tomorrow . . .'

'– No, really . . . I'm fine.'

There is a kind of sympathy that leaves the sufferer exhausted.

The word 'night' means 'I know what you're going through', but also '. . . and it is important to respond in the right way'. John's concern is not just to condole, but to help us bear pain creatively.

We saw that the experience of our weakness can lead us to an admission: that we are not our own saviours. Then, following the broad pattern of the books of *Night*, we saw that darkness can herald the approach of God, cleaving us off ourselves, opening us to himself. That can apply in prayer, and at depths of intensity we might scarcely think possible. But the pattern fits well too around the irritations that tense the most everyday lives.[1] These experiences are painful, confusing, feel unacceptable, and such feelings can be rightly owned. But, for night to be *dichosa*, blessed, there needs also, at some level, to be a 'yes'.

To get a sense of this, we might think, on the one hand, of a tendency from which we have longed to be free – those ingrained weaknesses which *Night* so skilfully exposed. It might be anger; or a crippling shyness; or a distorting lust; or the constant referral of everything to myself as the centre of pity or praise. We beg God to set us free. 'But I know he won't; it is too deep, and it has swooped up from nowhere too often before.' Change feels impossible, and the hope of release can just tail off into despair.

On the other hand, we might think of negative happenings, which grate or sting or ache. They are not our doing (they come like night) and they together comprise the downside of life: embarrassments, insults, a put-down; the company of people who excel at the one thing I felt good at myself; the humiliation of failure or rejection. These are disconcerting, and if we joked them off at the start, and felt strong enough to ride them, we can come to feel crushed, with the risk of growing bitter.

We put a lot of emotional energy into those two areas: personal weaknesses, from which we long to be free; negative situations which come uninvited upon us. Left like that, they are a recipe for despair in the weakness and resentment at what hurts us.

To leaving it like that, 'night' suggests an alternative. When the negative comes upon you, then *remember* your desire to be free – free from the personal weakness which was crippling you. It is here that God is doing it, and it is important not to panic, or run away.

Suppose, then, we get no thanks after going out of our way to help. The spontaneous reaction is to sting inside and make that 'the last time I ever do anything for *them*'. That is a time to recall the longing we may have had to grow out of our narrowness and sensitivity; and to thank God for this.

It is right of course to grieve, to take a stand, and to seek a remedy. But it is important too not to miss the God-content in the darkness. On offer is freedom from ourselves, for a God who fills. To trust – that God is present in this – can turn the pain, where there has to be pain, from death-throes into the pangs of birth.

Trust is the key to growth. One of John's images for growth is a mountain climb – *The Ascent of Mount Carmel*. But close reading reveals that his mountain, like Elijah's Carmel in Israel, like Moses' Horeb in Sinai, is a religious mountain. It speaks of communion, where the goal is not to sink a solitary flag-pole into the summit, but to 'make an altar of oneself' there for 'a sacrifice of love'.[2]

A mountain climb can take various forms. One approach is to seek a secure grip and a clear view before any step is taken. This is slow. As the cliff face becomes more hostile, fear tends to drain off one's adrenalin and make any progress increasingly wooden. Then, sooner or later, it will probably break down altogether: 'I'm stuck – and feel very small!'

There is another approach – and that kind of impasse may force us to it. It is to trust the directions and take the hand of someone higher up.

So with the night climb up Mount Carmel. One can seek absolute security before any next step. That makes life slow, fearful, and sooner or later the process will probably break down. Growth means a shift on to another's resources: taking another's hand, and trusting that, though I may now not see, the other sees.

The journey, if it is out of self into an unknown God, could not really progress in any other way. But our instinct for survival, coupled with the anxiety of our age for achievement and perceived meaning, conspire to make such a shift uniquely difficult.

John's own writing can work against him too: his system and schemas could make one mistake him for a spiritual cartographer, whose concern is to map each twist in the road and reduce unknowns to a minimum. But more original to him than schemas for growth is his witness to the vitality of God. He gives us the schemas, not to help us to predict, but to encourage us to surrender.

Some of his schemas – signs of contemplative prayer,[3] steps of love[4] – are clear instances of borrowing. They are helpful; but his own voice rings more truly in his conviction, 'You will not delay, if I do not fail to hope.'[5]

Address, then, what can be addressed – escape from Toledo, take the sad person for a walk in the hills, be extravagant in care for the sick. Recover the sparkle that enlivened relationships, projects, and prayer. Look as well into any infidelity that may be sapping the buoyancy of our journey. Do that. But there is a darkness which is not the result of infidelity and may not be removed by an effort to pull oneself together.

In such a case, John's invitation continues, do not struggle for something you once had and have now gone beyond. Instead, 'take heart, persevere patiently, without pain; trust in God' in 'loving attentiveness'.

That summarises his 'yes' to a God who 'never abandons those who seek him': a refusal to panic ('persevere'); the sense not to suffer unduly ('without pain'); shifting to another's resources ('trust in God') and to a new way of communicating ('in loving attentiveness').[6] Each element in the formula deserves attention.

## 'Persevere'

When our sources of energy seem to run dry, the natural question is, 'What have I done wrong?' or, 'What do I now have to do?'

Maybe I do not have to 'do' anything; at least, there may not be some key which, if I discover it, will unlock it all. Night rests on the reality of an involved God – and what I have to 'do' is not run away.

This bites into our nomadic culture, inclined as we are to move on when difficulties arise. This (a life of tourism, the level of sense) may assuage some types of pain, but it will ultimately produce a generation forgetful of what it is like to be still. John has a problem with people who 'spend their lives changing vocation, changing their lifestyle', never staying in one spot long enough to 'enter into the living reality' within them.[7] To love faithfully for a month is good. To love faithfully for thirty years is also good and, presumably, different – with a difference that only the person who has done it can know. For John, the very act of not running away is an exciting event.

### 'Without pain'

When something afflictive happens – like leaving people we love for an alien environment – there is a real danger of folding in on oneself. Pain does that, and the temptation is to look for a both/and: both staying with the new setting, and feeding on nostalgia for the old one. Unhappily, this both/and tends to backfire. One cannot both indulge self-pity and make the most of a new situation. If we approach the new on condition that others acknowledge our worth and soothe us, we may never see the opportunities the new genuinely offers. There is a choice between saying 'yes' to the self-pity, and staying curled up, or saying 'yes' to the future, and letting the past go. John calls the latter, 'letting yourself be carried by God'. The alternative brings unnecessary sadness:

> 'Although God does carry them, since he can do so without their involvement, they do not accept his guidance. In resisting God, who is carrying them, they make less headway on the journey, merit less, since they do not apply their wills, and in this very thing they suffer more.'[8]

Sometimes the new threatens too much that is precious to us to allow a simply buoyant choice for the future. In his final persecution, John himself could be quite laconic. Describing in a letter how he and his community would thresh the chickpeas they had harvested, he commented, 'It is lovely to handle these mute creatures – better than being mishandled by living ones!'[9] Pain can be too undermining to allow anything buoyant at all. But it helps if we do not suffer unduly, and one's inner peace may need a decision, or several decisions, not to. It may require, not solitary heroics, but a choice for the other's hand, and a leap, perhaps several leaps, on to a different life-vision.

'I have had to leave friends and it feels lonely and empty . . .'

'It is God who has brought you here. It is because he loves you, and he knows what is best for you. Can you trust that?'

## 'Trust', in 'loving attentiveness'

In the fourth gospel, Jesus shows himself anxious about his disciples' future suffering. They will be excommunicated, even killed. Jesus knows this; but his anxiety is not that they will suffer – that will happen, and he does not suggest a way of avoiding it. His anxiety is that they may panic, collapse inside, 'stumble' in their faith (cf. John 16: 1–2). Hence Jesus' most frequent exhortation is not 'Escape', but 'Do not be afraid'.

John of the Cross has transcribed this response of trust as: 'let yourselves be carried by God'. It sounds lovely. But it is letting oneself be carried 'by God'; and that can feel like the greatest effort.

As in practice learning to swim means letting go of the side of the pool, so trusting in God may in practice be experienced as risking the loss of all else. We may have to live as if he sustained us, in order to discover that he does sustain us.

We said that, while John speaks of the 'passive' night, passive and active run together. Indeed, his 'active night' (2–3 *Ascent*) discusses the handling of supernatural experiences that are certainly not of one's own doing; whereas the 'passive night' (1–2 *Night*) involves facing hardships which can require all our resources if we are not to be destroyed by them. Trust in the face of failure or betrayal, fidelity when the partner is drunk or abusive, integrity in a lie-ridden work-place; these are 'letting oneself be carried *by God*'. In a sense it means doing nothing other than remaining; but, like standing firm when the wind has reached gale force, it can feel like the greatest effort.

It is easy to let oneself be merely 'carried', when, for instance, prayer seems fruitless. Then it is easy to say: 'There's no need to be meticulous. Prayer is not about clock-watching – ten minutes less, fifteen, that's fine . . . anyway, somebody's got to do the work . . .' But to let oneself be carried 'by God' is not to run away from the emptiness, and to let it disclose a deeper communion. John calls it the level of 'pure spirit', where God is 'communicating himself to the soul',[10] a simpler attentiveness meeting a more total gift.

When a person or community loses initial appeal, it is easy to be just 'carried'. As the buoyancy or feeling yields to boredom or clashes of opinion, it is easy to be mesmerised by alternatives ('at least those others appreciate me!') or to hanker after a false euphoria ('we seemed so much happier at the start'). To let oneself be carried 'by God' is not to run from the loneliness but to let it disclose a deeper basis for togetherness: not a honeymoon basis, a golden wedding basis.

We spoke of Thérèse of Lisieux. For her, this togetherness meant a silver thread of naked trust, with the absolute minimum of feed-back. Poems which she composed during her months of inner darkness gave no hint of the seeming godlessness of it all. Explaining the brightness of her verses, she said, 'I sing *what I will to believe*.'[11] To go forward on that basis was for her to let herself be, not merely 'carried', but carried by God.

We detailed also John's final disgrace. Being just carried would have meant keeping quiet as policies changed ('They are, after all, wise and holy men'). To be carried by God meant remaining in the truth, and showing his teeth when he felt the truth was challenged. His companion, Juan Evangelista, recounts how John began to write letters of complaint.

> 'I remember one of them especially. It was so strong that, when I read it, I tried to get him not to send it, because of the trouble it would stir up – but he would not agree. He said that as a council member he was obliged to send it; and it would please God.'[12]

As in his life, so in his ministry, John retained the same watchword – let it be God who carries you. His departure from Granada meant a painful upheaval for the servant girl Juana. She seems to have lost her nerve and started looking for affirmation from any spiritual guide on hand to give it. John's response was caring, and clear. 'It seems to you that God is failing you. But nothing is failing you. You don't need to go off seeking advice.' To keep asking questions: that was to let herself be 'carried'. Yet all she had been told by John

had not suddenly become invalid. To be carried by God meant not
panicking in the lack of support, but allowing it to bring her to a
new level of maturity.

> 'The person who desires nothing but God does not walk in
> darkness, however dark and poor she may be in her own sight
> . . . You are doing well. Let it be, and be glad. Who are you
> to guide yourself? Wouldn't that end up fine!'[13]

John's vision, which can go into a phrase or stretch across a book,
is present here: an inflow of God; the darkness which is space for
the gift; and the faith which welcomes his entry.

Another letter puts it perfectly.[14] It addresses a nun, Leonor
de San Gabriel. Leonor felt isolated and confused. She had been
transferred by the religious authorities (of which John was one)
from a community she loved in Sevilla to one she was less sure
about in distant Córdoba. Her vow of religious obedience obliged
her, but she was having difficulty bringing her heart into line.
To help her, John is not above a touch of flattery at the end of
the letter.

> 'As you are so well seasoned in years, and have such experience,
> you know well the kind of thing that happens in these [new]
> foundations; that is why we chose your Reverence. If it were
> just a matter of finding nuns, there are so many up here that
> there isn't room for them all!'

Whatever of the persuasion, John's tenderness takes him deeper.
It is not men, he says, but God who has done this. Ostensibly,
that is untrue: it *is* men; men who know little of Leonor's life and
whose decision could seem fairly arbitrary. Yet John perceives the
loving mother of the grace of God sustaining Leonor even through
that, using even that to nurture her. So it is God doing it. God is
doing it because he has a gift: himself, his 'company'; and for the
gift there must be space – here, Leonor's solitude. But for the gift
to enter she must say 'yes' to the gift in the darkness. The letter
goes like this:

> 'Jesus be in your soul, my daughter in Christ.
>     Thanks indeed for your letter; and thanks be to God for
> wanting to make use of you in this foundation. It is His Majesty

who has done this, to bring you greater profit. For the more he wants to give, the more he makes us desire, till he leaves us empty so as to fill us with blessings . . . God's immense blessings can only fit into a heart that is empty. They come in that kind of solitude. For this reason, the Lord would love to see you, since he loves you well, well and truly alone, intent on being himself all your company.'

That is the gift – his company – in the space these very human circumstances can create – her solitude. But then the response of faith:

'. . . intent on being himself all your company.
   And your Reverence will have to take heart and be content only with his company, in order to find all contentment in that; for even if a person were in heaven, if she didn't align her will to want it, she wouldn't be content.'

That is what turns pain into night: grieve, address what can be addressed, do not condone the sin that may be causing the situation; but trust that the Father holds this situation in his hands, and will turn it to blessing.

'Do not be afraid': the command makes sense because night tempts one to be, precisely, afraid. Afraid to say 'yes' to a one-way path that may end in wasteland; Leonor's fear of unknown Córdoba over comfortable Sevilla; the spouse's or celibate's fear of being left on an emotional shelf; the disciple's fear of making a gift, and not being filled. As we have said, it is not that one would necessarily choose another path, but one may never fully choose this one.

John has traced a pattern – a God who gives himself, a darkness making room for the gift – which presents a purpose worthy of a person's life. But his promise of encounter is not reserved for those who make it to the end. John sees the pattern available now – present in faith, guaranteed in Jesus, released in prayer. Having reviewed the pattern, we want next to take hold of this encounter. Not that there will be no pain or confusion; but there is a precious and more significant friendship, closer than pain or confusion. That is a valid reason not to be afraid.

# PART V – Encounter

## *15: The Experience of God (I)*

'Little children, you are of God, and have overcome them; for he who is in you is greater than he who is in the world.'[1] It seems that what gave the early Christians courage to persevere was not a secure future, but the certainty of a companionship more powerful than anything the future could bring.

So with John of the Cross: when he says 'night', what comes to his mind is not so much suffering, even redeemed suffering, as presence.

He knows this presence to be worth the sacrifice. His doctrine has been directing us to it: a God who gives himself (*Flame*); the space we make for the gift (*Ascent*); the opening God himself carves for his gift (*Night*); a project which stretches from God's plan in eternity to its final fulfilment in heaven (*Canticle*). For all their difference in genre, the books, in tracing this pattern, use a common language: they all speak of love; or of faith; or ('these three theological virtues go forward together'[2]) of faith, hope and love. Believe, trust, love, and you are receiving the gift. These form the meeting place; they *are* the encounter. That encounter in faith, hope and love is the theme of the next two chapters.

In fact much of what has been said up to now describes faith and love in action. If, given another chance to assert myself over others, I instead resist the urge to dominate, allow the others to be themselves, and say to God, 'I don't need that; I need you', that is love. If someone on whose example my belief had depended, ups and abandons the gospel they had taught me to embrace, and I none the less cling on to it, that is faith. If, in the face of a deep-seated defect, I do not allow cynicism ('It will never change') to close doors on the future, that is hope.

Here we want not so much to develop on the practice of faith-hope-love, as to show its inner vitality. This, by giving meaning to a statement of John's, and by answering a contemporary question.

The statement is rather startling:

> 'the Christian should realise that the value of her good works,
> fasts, alms, penances, prayers, etc., does not depend so much
> on their quantity or *quality*, but on the *love* of God which she
> brings to them . . .'3

More starkly, 'What is the use of anything, what value has
anything, except the *love* of God?'4

Well, love does make people more bearable, and a cheerful giver
is better than a gloomy giver, but at the end of the day things have
to be done, and better done unlovingly than not done at all. Yet,
says John uncompromisingly, love alone gives value. That requires
some explanation.

As for our question, it is perennial, but has today a specially
urgent ring. The question is: Where can I find an experience
of God?

'Give me an experience of God!' It is sometimes said against an
ethical code, a religion of correct behaviour; or against allegiance
to an institutional church. There may be need for education in the
'over againsts'. Scripture shows a God whose love makes demands
on the way people behave, and a community happy to institute
structures to support their faith and mission. But in itself, the
demand is legitimate enough: give me an experience of God –
and not some substitute.

John of the Cross shared the anxiety. It is where he started:
'Where have you hidden?' Where can I find you; you, and not some
substitute? Only God, personally, could meet his real need.

When John seeks an 'experience of God', he says what he
intends by experience. He does not mean 'feeling' as opposed to
'not feeling'; he means 'reality' as opposed to 'mere theory'. He
is not looking for a shot in the arm to brighten a dreary day; he is
looking for a person, with whom he is content to be, even if the day
stays dreary. He assured us of God's willingness to 'communicate
himself', and added 'at least in a hidden way'.5 His search, then,
is not for a *feeling* of encounter, but for encounter. But, given that
proviso, our contemporary question is his own: he wants, not just
perfection, but nothing less than 'union'. 'Give me an experience
of God.'

That forces him – him especially – into an impossible dilemma.

One horn of the dilemma is this: the God whom John seeks is, for him, utterly beyond. He stresses this in a culture apt to trivialise the realm of the divine:

> 'It amazes me to see what goes on nowadays. Anyone who does twopence worth of meditation, if they reach a certain quietness and are aware of a train of inner words, baptises it all as coming from God, and thinks that's how it is. They say, 'God said to me'; 'I got this answer from God'; and it isn't that at all . . .'[6]

However, John says that God is beyond, not only because people he directed needed to be reminded of that, but because that was the terrible truth he came increasingly to know.

If put to it, he would divide reality into two. On the one hand, there is the universe of stars and space, sun and earth; of animals and plants; of microbes, neutrinos and quarks. There is spirit, flesh, thought and movement. There are people, with all our relationships, and all the choices and chances holding our history together. In short: everything there is, on the one hand.

On the other hand, there is God.

God, who is not a part of all of that, who is not one more piece when all the other pieces have been located; God, who sustains all of that but is grasped by none of it. All of that derives from, exists in, points to, reveals God, but when one has penetrated to the deepest godliness of it all, God remains infinitely different. '"God" means just what man cannot say, that blazing reality which is and remains for us the absolute mystery.'[7]

In seeking a name for the encounter with God which heaven will involve, John sifts the scriptures, and finds in the Apocalypse and Psalms several images which tell us 'something'. They all frame it well, but, he says, 'none of them explains it, nor all of them together'.[8] God remains to be named when we have named all that can be named. 'Of God himself', John told us, 'nothing could be said that would be like him.'[9]

This God is utterly beyond; yet – the other horn of the dilemma – John has an absolute need to encounter him. We saw this red raw in Toledo, but it is present throughout his writings. His exultant view of the human person demands it.

John was writing at a time (1578–91) when Spain's empire, and with that, the optimism of its writers, was on the verge of decline. The Renaissance view of the greatness of Man was turning a little yellow at the edges. Enjoy it while you can, but soon it will turn 'to dirt, to dust, to smoke, to shadow, to nothing', says the poet Góngora (1561–1627), neatly conveying the mood.[10]

Against that, John has no doubt about humanity's real possibilities for greatness. The universe is 'a limitless sea of love';[11] the soul, 'a most beautiful and finely wrought image of God';[12] a single thought of a human person 'worth more than all the world'.[13] There is no question about John's optimism. It is just that it translates into an equivalent hunger when human capacity is not felt to be filled:

> 'The capacity of these caverns [the human spirit] is deep, because that which can fill them is deep, infinite; and that is God. So in a sense their capacity will be infinite; so their thirst is infinite, and their hunger is deep and infinite, and their sense of pain and disintegration is infinite death' when the soul is alert to 'receive what will fill it.'[14]

That is the dilemma: John has an absolute need for a God who transcends absolutely. The impasse accounts for most of the deviations in human living – trying to fill the need with something else, or trivialising God so that I can grasp him. John however believes that there is an answer which compromises nothing.

First we are told where 'an experience of God' is not; at least, not certainly. A feeling of dryness does not prove God's absence. A feeling of holy warmth does not prove his presence. The reality of God is, simply, deeper. To quote one expression of this:

> 'You do very well [. . .] to seek him always as one hidden. You honour God greatly and indeed come near to him, when you hold him to be nobler and deeper than anything you can attain. So do not settle down or try to find a corner in what your mind and heart can grasp . . . And do not be like many heartless people who have a low opinion of God: they think that when they cannot understand him or sense or feel him, he is further away – when the truth is more the opposite: it is when you understand him less clearly that you are coming closer to him . . . So you do well at all times, whether life, or faith, is smooth, or hard, you do well to hold God as hidden, and so to cry out to him, "Where have you hidden?"'[15]

Feeling he is absent need not mean he is absent; feeling he is closer need not mean he is closer. Having disconnected ninety-five per cent of the gauges we use to read God's proximity in our life, John does have something positive to say:

'If you want to hear it again, listen to a word filled with reality and unfathomable truth. It is this: *seek him in faith and love.*'[16]

Here the dilemma is resolved. John is looking for union with a transcendent God: he needs a means which yet does not get in the way; a ladder which is also the top of the ladder. Believing, hoping, loving are the only means, and they are the means by which a person is directly 'united' with God.

John's statements are clear:

'The more faith the soul has, the more is she united with God.'[17] Again, 'the more hope the soul has, the greater her union with God.'[18]

Other experiences 'are not a means which would unite the soul with God; only charity does this.'[19]

'The soul's health is the love of God.'[20]

In emphasising this (each of his books does emphasise it) John undercuts the accretions with which later theologians would encumber the spiritual itinerary. In reckoning faith, hope and love, open to everyone, as far more significant than supernatural phenomena, he cuts through, too, the esotericism of his own pietistic age. Do not set store by such phenomena, visions, inner words, 'because all that they are in themselves cannot help one in the love of God as much as the smallest act of living faith and hope made in emptiness and renunciation of all'.[21] In other words, believe in the God who has revealed himself in Jesus Christ: that is the most real event; take on board other experiences only insofar as they point to and rest within that event of faith.[22]

John writes this with a theologian's security; and with a pastor's sense of what works in practice. So in his letters, when he wanted to say something that would help, it was this that he said:

'Live only in dark and genuine faith, and sure hope, and unmitigated love . . . Be joyful, and trust in God.'[23]

'Live in faith and hope, even though it be in darkness, since in this darkness it is God who supports the soul. Cast your care on God, since he has care of you. He won't forget you . . .'[24]

For John himself, there was life here, fresh air, relief when his circumstances were choking him. Confrère and biographer Alonso testifies how, when his brethren were hassling John into an increasingly tight corner, faith let him find God there and gave him room to breathe:

> 'One indication that the servant of the Lord [John of the Cross] had this kind of faith was seeing him in the suffocating trials he went through . . . [His faith] gave him strength, opening doors for him so that he could draw breath in the presence of his God, even when the pathways seemed to be completely closed.'[25]

Whether as theologian, as pastor, or in his personal life, John kept coming back to believing, hoping, loving. He holds that this puts people in contact with nothing less than God.

## Faith, hope, and love give you God

There is something strange about John's description of these Christian responses.

In the way his antecedents spoke of them, the emphasis was on launching out, thrusting towards the divine. Yet when John starts talking, the emphasis is negative. His stress is not on launching out, but on letting go; not on grasping, but on 'the nakedness and emptiness there is in faith and hope and love of God'.[26]

So in books two and three of *Ascent*, John lists the insights and lights brightening the mind, and the sources of pleasure, even religious pleasure, enlivening the heart – only to say that a loving faith may require us to go beyond them. Again, he defines love as aligning our will perfectly with God's; but in practice, that means not aligning it with anything else.[27] At its bluntest, the journey consists – 'I really want to persuade religious people' of this – 'not in a multiplicity of thoughts and procedures and fresh angles and feelings – though all of this may in its own way be necessary early on – but in one thing only: knowing how to deny yourself truly . . . for Christ.'[28]

The negative thrust is startling. How do we interpret it?

Partly, it offers protection. Sitting loose to what boosts us means our faith need not collapse, if the boost fails. A sense of inner peace, or of contact with a higher world, or of admiration for

an inspiring person, or of fellowship within a group: these are
good. But none of them is God, and a refusal to pin all our hope
on them shields us from unnecessary sorrow. The people or the
feelings can change. They can turn out to be partial, skin-deep, or
erroneous.

John lived in a culture which delighted in the extraordinary.
It seems to have made him uneasy. Visions, raptures, messages,
fragrances, saints, devils, angels, God – it was all there in one
gloriously pious mix; and one kink in people's motivation could
leave them hopelessly mixed up.[29] In practice, self-deception and
self-projection were rife:

> 'They'll be thinking it was all rather special, and that God had
> spoken; and it will have been little more than nothing, or
> nothing, or less than nothing. Because if something does not
> give birth to humility, and love, and dying to self, and godly
> simplicity, and silence – what can it be?'[30]

Into that, John fed the principles he was formulating in the *Ascent*:
what unites you to God is faith, hope, love, in Christ, risen in his
Church, present in his word. Anything else 'that you could imagine
or understand or think in this life', while it may be good if it stirs up
your faith and love, in itself 'is not and cannot be a direct means to
union with God'.[31]

So John's negative emphasis in faith and love is prudent enough:
unhook a chain of dependence which can lead to tragedy. Still, in
itself it could be depressing, even destructive.[32] However, the fact
is that John is saying 'Let go, get out of the way', only because he
is so convinced that God, in his truth and love, is pressing to come
in. His God is not 'out there' to be hit upon by the lucky voyager;
his God is invasive, self-giving, entering to befriend. Where the gift
is *that* total and immediate, then making room, not launching out,
has to be priority. It has consequences:

> 'Because the role of these three [faith, hope, love] is to withdraw
> the soul from all that is less than God, *consequently* they *unite*
> her with God.'[33]

The whole pattern of John's experience is concentrated here:
making 'room for God in order to receive';[34] 'when the soul
makes room for God, then she is enlightened and transformed in

God'.[35] This is a 'letting go' born of passion more than prudence. It is the scramble of people who realise that a loved one whom they thought to be in a distant country, has already got into the lift and will be coming through *that* door in a matter of seconds.

Paul's understanding of love – 'poured into our hearts through the Holy Spirit who has been given to us' (Rom. 5:5) – was taken into the decrees of the Council of Trent in northern Italy (1545–63), decrees promulgated in Salamanca while John was a student there. They effectively spoke of faith, hope and love as gifts of God given in baptism, by which God, dwelling in the soul of the Christian, takes us into his own inner life.[36]

Developing on this, faith is a divine gift by which we believe God as he proposes himself; love, a gift by which we choose God and want what he wants. In this, the Spirit of God is loving us and putting us in the current of love between the Son and the Father. By faith we know with the Son's knowing and by charity we love with the Spirit's loving.

Something takes place in the Christian which is greater than she is: faith is God lifting the soul into God's own life. It is 'theological' virtue: it comes from God (*theos*) and leads to God.

This is not a depth one necessarily perceives – though in mystical experience it is beginning somehow to register. But this (grace, the indwelling of God in the soul, the soul's sharing the life of God, faith–hope–love) is a Christian's deepest truth.

The impact of God upon him lets John see this with new eyes. With those eyes he reads our response. Where God is this close, our response has to be at root a receiving; and that receiving cannot but put us in contact with such a God. 'No one can say "Jesus is Lord" except by the Holy Spirit' (1 Cor. 12:3). Put otherwise, say 'Jesus is Lord', and you will already have been acted upon by the Spirit of God. Believe, hope, love, and you are receiving God.

John's own experience of God nerved him to speak in this way, because it was experience in faith – 'most enlightened faith', *Flame* says – not outside faith.[37] Contemplative growth, into the white heat of a dark, loving knowledge, is growth into faith, not into something foreign to faith.[38] John's security remains, not science or elation, but belief in the God of Jesus Christ. In summoning the believer to 'union', he proposes a goal which, while it must unfold, is already ours.

John has some quite magical ways of putting this, and we shall look at them next. But his dilemma, an absolute need for a transcendent God, is here resolved. Faith, hope, love are not our attempt to colonise the divine realm; they are God adopting us into his life. Where God is a God who reveals and gives, to believe and to love *is* to encounter him.

# 16: The Experience of God (II)

In John's dictionary, 'faith, hope, love' translate commitment – above all, God's to us. Focusing now on each of these gifts specifically, we shall find that divine commitment expressed in a compelling way.

### 'The abyss of faith'

'Here we live by faith.' It tends to conjure up a sense of grey distance, which some people are lucky enough to have pierced by a flash of mystical lightning; for the majority, it is a case of soldiering on.

Yet when John says: 'Faith, not phenomena', it is not because he wants us to get used to surviving on rations. It is because faith is fullness, and phenomena are less than fullness.

Faith, believing the word of God, believing 'into' God, is living contact. In it the Spirit communicates not words, but, personally, the Word. 'In faith: that is where the Holy Spirit will shed most light.' One's insights or experiences give some light; but compared with the encounter in faith, they are, John says, as tin to gold, and as a drop to the ocean: they give the person wisdom 'about one or two or three truths; but in this [attentiveness in faith], *all* the Wisdom of God is communicated to her in a total way – that is, *the Son of God*, who is *communicated to the soul in faith*.'[1] Our faith is the Spirit's aligning us with the pulse of the Son of God.

In this case, faith comes across not as grey distance, but as *light*.

John had inherited this definition: faith is 'an aptitude of the soul, certain and obscure'.[2] He accepts that: it is an aptitude (not a one-off, but a gift by which to live), it is certain (as certain as the word of God), and it is obscure (because in delivering truth it does not deliver proof).

Yet when John develops, 'light' is the word that keeps recurring. 'How wonderful it was: the pillar of cloud, though it was dark, illumined the night' for Israel; so faith 'illumines and gives light' to the soul.[3]

It is dark because it gives too much light, an 'excess' of light.[4] You can look freely at the stars, but look at the sun and it will blind you; you can pick out features at a distance, but if the object is eye-close, you cannot focus. So when God is communicating himself to the soul, the mind's natural field of vision has too narrow a range, and we have to engage by believing, not by focusing. Were faith to open us merely to a world of sharper ideas or more vivid impressions, then its light would indeed look bright. As it opens us to God, its light blinds us.

Faith, then, is dark, not because God is distant, but because he is eye-close, soul-close. In faith is God, 'communicating himself to the soul'.[5]

John has charming ways of putting this. As his mind was steeped in Scripture, biblical images are the ones that tend to surface when he is rummaging for words. One image concerns Gideon's attack on the Midianites. The book of Judges has Gideon and his men sneaking up to the enemy camp with blazing torches hidden inside jars. When the men surround the camp, the moment has come: they smash the jars, raise the torches, and shout, 'A sword for the Lord and for Gideon!' (Judg. 7:20).

'So faith, symbolised by those jars, contains in itself the light of God.'[6] Whatever of the physics in Gideon's case, John is clear that the jar of faith keeps the divine light inside blazing. It does not just refer to the light, or wait for the light, or substitute for the light; it contains the light – God-light. When we die, the jars will smash and we shall see the light; as it is, the light is hidden, but, through believing, we *possess* the light. If we want vision, felt evidence, manifestation, then faith will be frustrating; if we want the reality, then faith, alone, gives us an experience of God.

*Canticle* says the same, in its love-song idiom. After the bride cries, 'Where?', a long search ensues. She goes up and down hills and valleys, appeals to the shepherds and questions creation, makes a thorough nuisance of herself and complains bitterly, until, finally, she is forced back to her original, truest resource: 'she does not know what to do, except to return to faith itself', as to that which 'holds and enshrouds the face, the beauty of her Beloved.'

O fount like crystal –
if only on your silvered-over face
those eyes I long for so
might suddenly appear;
I bear their portrait sketched upon my heart! (Stanza 12).

A spring of water, welling up, a fountain spreading out into a sunlit pond which reflects the bright sky on its surface; 'silvered-over'.[7]

The image shifts to a silver-plated vase, silver plating gold within. The silver, we are told, is like the propositions of faith – what we believe, the articles of the creed, the words of the gospel. But when John says 'faith gives you God', he does not mean only that faith gives you correct information about God. Faith gives us God, the living God, and the propositions are like markings getting us to stand in the right place for the gift. So if faith is silver-plated (the creed), the plated vase delivers the gold (the reality). There will be no need to profess the creed in heaven. Heaven will scrape off the plating and we shall see the gold. Here, what we see is the silver, but it *contains the gold*. It 'holds and enshrouds' the face of the Beloved.

Paul has it: 'If you confess with your lips that Jesus is Lord and believe with your heart that God raised him from the dead' (the propositions), 'you will be saved' (the reality) (Rom. 10.9).

Faith-silver enshrouding faith-gold. We are left, then, with this mind-bending phrase: 'faith gives us God himself, communicates him, but plated over by faith.'[8]

## Healing the memory with hope

John shows himself aware that believing, hoping and loving are a total response of the whole person; aware too that our faculties – mind, memory, and will – are not three 'things', but the act of the human person in three aspects (understanding, remembering, desiring).[9] He is holistic.

That said, it still serves him to analyse and connect. In doing so, he relates faith to the mind (knowing as the Son knows), love to the will (loving in the Spirit's love). Hope goes with memory.

Memories are made of – what? I 'remember' visiting Scotland as a child. I 'remember' writing a letter yesterday. 'Memory' tends to mean that by which I recall to mind events of the past – 'painful memories', 'happy memories'.

We need these memories to know who we are, to know our place. People who lose their memory are painfully handicapped in this area. From that, though, memory appears not just as an archive of past images, but as the person's facility for recall, a facility which holds her together in the flux of time.

When John says 'memory', he means it essentially like this: the person's capacity to retrieve, anticipate, possess the otherwise fleeting moment as her own; the faculty, then, of possession, of self-possession, roughly corresponding to what we mean by 'consciousness'. It gives me my place vis-à-vis the past, but also with a view to the present (the soul can 'remember [what] it lacks'), or to the future (remembering death, remembering heaven).[10] It is what lets me be myself in time.

Non-existent though past and future may be, their influence is real enough. The past in particular sinks roots into the psyche, and, as time passes, accumulates influence over the mind and emotions. It feeds aggression or lust or pride.[11]

John is himself masterfully aware ('and this is something we are constantly experiencing')[12] of how the roots from the past can tyrannise the emotions; and of how the future can paralyse with worry one's fluidity in the here and now.[13]

'Night' – especially as passive, as what God does in us – is a healing of the memory. It does not destroy our impressions: these are good, and can awaken us to the good.[14] It does however challenge their dominance over our present freedom. Night sets us free from enslavement to 'was' or to 'may be'.

The programme includes its active aspect – what we do. Get used to unhooking your self from 'memories' (inflammatory images of past events, worrying expectations of the future) and let your 'memory' be free to possess fully the present. This unhooking is the work of 'hope'.

'Do not be anxious about tomorrow, for tomorrow will be anxious for itself. Let the day's own trouble be sufficient for the day' (Matt. 6:34). Or as Mark Twain reputedly said, 'I have suffered very many things in my life. Most of them never happened!' John too is eminently practical, if a little clinical.

'The build-up of anxiety or worry which problems and crises can cause a person in no way helps to bring about a better situation; rather, it normally makes matters worse, and harms the person herself . . . It is obviously never any help getting anxious . . . To bear it all with calm, peace, tranquillity, not only opens her to many blessings; it also helps her, in these difficulties themselves, to come to a better decision and to apply a remedy that will actually do some good.'[15]

During building work on the friary at Córdoba, one wall needed to be demolished, and the workmen attempted to direct its fall. The engineering back-fired; the masonry fell instead on to one of the rooms, which collapsed under the impact. It was John's room, and friars and builders rushed to the scene, shifting the rubble, expecting to find a 5′3″ corpse underneath. They finally unearthed John, huddled in a corner, 'laughing'![16]

Collapsing walls apart, self-possession does seem to have been one of John's fortes. But his freeing the memory from 'what happened', 'what might happen' or even 'what decidedly is happening', is not just a step towards mental health. Hope is negatively a refusal to get locked on to anxiety or passion, because there is positively a reality in the present which infinitely eclipses those motivations. Hope releases the soul's fluidity not just 'from', but 'for' – for what is really meant to fill it. And that is God.[17]

John knows only two realities: the present, and eternity. Hope pulls memory off the suction pads of yesterday and tomorrow, and cups it upwards in the present. 'The sacrament of the present moment', it has been called. Eternity is bearing down, like an inverted triangle, upon one point in time only: now.

Worry in this sense is not just a pain; it is a tragedy, because it absorbs in something less what is meant for something greater. Hope means easing the mind of what inflames it or frightens it, and cupping it upwards to the God who alone can fill it.

When John speaks of the Mother of Jesus, it is in this connection. She moved freely, refusing to let herself be paralysed by past or future. In her mountain climb, she renounced the need for pre-planned handholds, opting instead to surrender to the guidance, the hand of Another. Her hope set her free to be possessed fully in each present moment by 'the Holy Spirit'.[18]

As with faith, so with hope, John can emphasise a letting-go, in this case of past and future, only because he is convinced that God is hovering, pressing, to come in and fill the gap. And he will fill it: 'Where God is concerned' – and only there – 'hope attains as much as it hopes for.'[19]

It is worth trying when something embarrassing happens. One

is tempted to take refuge in the past – 'There have been occasions when I performed . . . magnificently – they are the real me!' Or in the future – 'I'm still learning; give me a year, and I'll show them!' Instead, 'hope' here means accepting the offer which the embarrassment is making, by standing, poor, in the present – and receiving my security (at last, for once) from God.

Another of John's letters puts his theory to the proof. It is to Leonor again (of Sevilla/Córdoba fame).[20] This time she is afraid of having upset the superior of her order, Nicolás Doria. Doria is an ambiguous figure, variously judged by history. But whatever of the thornier issues, it does seem clear that an upset in that camp was worth taking seriously. John was on the Council with Doria, well poised, then, to intervene. His reply to Leonor is tender (he is concerned about the damage stress may do to her health). It is also practical, addressing the issue in a thorough way. But it is ultimately theological: hope is in question; her relationship with God is at stake. The letter goes like this:

> 'Jesus be in your soul, my daughter in Christ.
>     On reading your letter I felt for you deeply, and it distresses me to see how you suffer, because of the way it can harm your spirit and even your health. You should know that you don't seem to me to have such grounds for anxiety – because, as far as I can see, our Father [Doria] isn't at all annoyed with you, and has completely forgotten the matter; and even if he hadn't, your apologies would undoubtedly have dispelled any antipathy; and if there is still any problem, I'll be careful to speak well of you. Have no anxiety, and think no more of it, for there is no reason to . . .'

That is part of the answer: what needs attending to gets attended to; today's own trouble is enough for today. But John says this above all because a memory that should be cupped upwards to God, in a hope that infallibly receives, is being trapped downwards by anxieties about what happened and what might happen. He goes on:

> '. . . and think no more of it, for there is no reason to. So I consider that it is certainly a temptation which the devil keeps bringing to *your memory*, so that what should be *occupied in God* be occupied in this . . .'

Ultimately, for John, the event which hope receives, which presses in on the present, is the risen Christ. He comes, in prayer, but always, to the poor of spirit who expect salvation only from him.

'Let the garden be closed then, without pain or worry, for he who entered bodily for his disciples, when the doors were closed, and gave them peace, without them knowing or imagining that this could be, nor how, will enter in spirit into the soul . . . and he will fill her with peace.'

So, 'let her not fail to pray, and let her hope, in nakedness and emptiness, for he who is good to her will not delay.'[21]

## The soul lives where it loves

Faith, hope, love are called 'theological virtues'. That can sound rather scientific. The term is accurate enough: we are speaking of 'virtue', a person's way of being, not an occasional fluke; and the virtue is 'theological', having its origin and end in God. The science, however, should not obscure the vitality of it all. When John says faith, hope, or here, love, he prefers to say it like this:

'One dark night/fired with love's urgent longing . . .'

This is John at his most real. His God is poetry. Love for his God, and for the people of his God, is John's passion. In some parts of his writing, John can be diffident, apologetic.[22] But in speaking of love, his confidence is absolute. He knows what he is talking about.

Love heals history, where the Spirit has power to turn every wound, even the wounds of sin, into 'wounds of love'.[23] Love decodes the meaning of the world, which John reads as 'a limitless sea of love engulfing him'.[24] He knows from the inside that love is life-blood: 'When the person has no love, she is dead.'[25] Love is John's area of expertise.

When he speaks of love he means Christian love, which goes beyond pay-offs. He has a poem (taken mostly from a popular ballad of his day) which pictures Christ as a young shepherd in love with a shepherdess. John added an extra stanza which shows what sacrifice love can exact. In it, the shepherd climbs a tree, spreads wide his 'fair arms', and dies there, 'his heart with love sore wounded'. It is a question of crucified love; the gift of self, to and for the other.[26]

Crucified though it may be, love as John knows it is not stoical or repressive. Here are some of his principles.

'Love likes to be strong, to touch with impetuous power.'

'Love is never idle; it is in continuous movement.'

'This is the nature of love: it can search through all that belongs to the loved one.'

'The true lover is content only when he employs all he himself is, all his worth, all he has and receives, in the service of the one he loves.'

'Love is its own payment.'[27]

It is on these terms that God, 'the principal lover', wants to be met:

'Blessed the soul who loves! God is her captive, submitting to her every wish. That is God's way: if you approach him with love and treat him well, you shall have him do whatever you want; but if you try some other way, you may as well keep quiet!'[28]

These are the findings of one who knows love from the inside. His description of the transformed soul is a description of himself: she becomes, he says, *'una maestra de amar'* – an expert in loving.[29]

About love, John makes two things very clear, and these are what we want to say here. One, that love is something God does; it is, first, his activity. And, two, that his love changes a person.

First, then, love – charity, the gift of baptism, the stuff of Christian life – is God's activity.

This was important for John in his last days when his own ability to love was being subjected to impossible demands. Faced with a campaign of libel from among his own brethren, and the antagonism of his superior as sickness took a hold, John stayed calm and forgiving. His letter bears repeating: it shows that the love he gave, he felt he received from God.

'Love greatly those who speak against you and do not love you, because in this way love will come to birth in a heart that has none. That is what God does with us: *he loves us*, that we might love him, *through the love he has for us*.'[30]

Love is God's activity: 'our' love like a kite, hanging in the wind of God's love for us.

This activity of God is called the Holy Spirit. He is the 'flame', the 'principal agent', the 'principal lover'. Love is first his gift of himself, disembarking into the soul. 'Hope does not disappoint us, because God's love has been poured into our hearts through the Holy Spirit who has been given to us' (Rom. 5:5).

Our love, for God or for God's creation, is the offspring of this outpouring. There is something of a double-take in this, where the Spirit comes in to give me the love which I need to let him in. Such love is a reciprocal event, as the suppleness of wax under the impress of a seal is both the condition and the result of the impress. So the Spirit-gift creates in me the capacity to receive the gift. Love is an activity of God.

It must be so if it does what John says it does: 'by love' the person 'is united with God'.[31] If God is truly beyond us, only God can unite us with God. Only if God were pouring in would anything we do help to join us to him. That is it: love is our Spirit-given 'yes' to an inpouring God.

'Give me an experience of God.' Turn to God present within you, and love him. You may not feel his presence; but want him, value him, give yourself to him, say yes to him, adore him. Love him, and you are experiencing God.

The *Flame* uses the language of 'centre' for this: not geographical centre, like pips in an orange, but personal centre, where all my energies converge. That centre is convex, turned out to another – hanging on another: 'the centre of the soul is God'. I am myself, when I am given to him. The 'Yes' of love centres me, unites me to him at my centre.

> 'It is by love that the soul is united with God . . . So for the person to be in her centre, which is God, it is sufficient for her to have one degree of love, because by just one degree the soul is united with him by grace.'[32]

The centre of the soul is God. That is how 'given', how impending he is. He is present where I am most myself, not geographically, but personally, tending himself in friendship. When I love, his love clasps me at my centre. It is primarily his activity.

Second, his love transforms.

John's last days proved the ultimate test of his belief in love's creative power. While he was being stonewalled or abused, he was telling his friends that love, alone, changes people. In the case of his antagonistic superior, Crisóstomo, who could excel at being awkward, the theory seems to have proved true. As John's life was slipping away, Crisóstomo wept at his bedside and begged his forgiveness. Love, put where there was none, did seem to have drawn love out. 'That is what God does with us: he loves us, that we might love him, through the love he has for us.'

Much that we have heard John say has its home here. When he spoke of disordered desire, he focused on its power to form and deform. Our desires make us as big or as small as their object.[33] Bad friends can make us bad, as Paul reminds the Corinthians (1 Cor. 15:33). But good company can make us good. And God's company, says John, does not rest till he makes us fit for his company. 'God's aim is to make us gods by participation, as he is God by nature – like fire turning everything to fire.'[34] In short, love does not just admire; it creates 'likeness'.[35]

It is that experience of meeting the eyes of someone who sees through us, but does not despise us, and whose eyes hold out the possibility of becoming more than we are. 'For God, to gaze is to love' – a gospel gaze which blazes its way into the person's heart. He does not simply look at the beautiful; his look makes a person beautiful.

> You looked with love upon me
> and deep within, your eyes imprinted grace;
> this mercy set me free,
> held in your love's embrace,
> to lift my eyes adoring to your face (*Canticle* stanza 32).

That is John's vision: a God, constantly gazing at the universe, personally meeting the eyes of each person in the universe, with a look that 'cleanses, makes beautiful, enriches and enlightens'. His love is creative: it elicits and forms – 'taking her and placing her in himself, making her like himself'. 'Our' love is a yes to that.[36]

Such is John's view of faith, hope, love: a being found, more even than a finding. This takes us back to the statement and the request with which we began these chapters.

The request was for encounter: 'Give me an experience of God.' John's answer is his own experience, of a God who, where we make room, fills it, and where we cannot, undertakes to create room so that he may fill it. While we viewed that as a night journey stretched across John's works and across a person's lifetime, it concentrates into now, in the act of believing, hoping, loving. These open the spirit to the God who will not fail to play his part, 'by communicating himself, at least in a hidden way'.[37]

Believe, hope, love, says John, and you are experiencing God.

The statement – that only love is of value – finds an explanation here too. Certainly, if it is *this* love, it is of value in a way nothing else could be.

The powerlessness of night brought an admission, that we need to be saved, and that we are not our own saviours. Into this, John announced the proximity of God, a God who loves to give himself, and whose love, in giving, transforms. The guarantee of this is God's fidelity to himself: 'he acts as God, to show who he is.'[38] Salvation is possible, because God makes it possible.

In that case, what is vital, for each person, and for the world, is that there should be people who make it their business to receive the gift. Love does that. As tent canvas drenched in rain needs only to be touched for the water to seep in, so a universe drenched in an outpoured Spirit needs only a touch, but it does need a touch, for the healing Spirit to seep in. Love, pure, disinterested, self-giving and self-forgetful love, is the touch. Love is thus a supreme value. It helps save the world.

> 'A little of this pure love is more precious to God, more precious for the soul, and of more benefit to the Church, even though it seems to be doing nothing, than all those other works put together . . . Since [in the Song of Songs] God adjures them not to wake the bride from this love, who would dare to do so and escape reprimand? – It is for this goal of love that we were created.'[39]

This invites us to take two remaining steps in sounding John's soul. So much is at stake in what he has said: encounter with a transforming God; change for people who feel incapable of change; salvation for a world in need of being saved. If faith, hope, love achieve this, where do we see them in act? We shall look at John's vision of prayer for an answer. But before we come to that, there is a more fundamental issue. With so much at stake, only Jesus could guarantee the authenticity of what John is saying. Given the terror of night, with its promise of union, where does Jesus fit in it all? John's vision depends on this. It is a question about Jesus.

# 17: A Question About Jesus

There is a moving scene towards the end of *A Man for All Seasons*, Robert Bolt's play about Sir Thomas More. Thomas is in prison, disgraced already and soon to be executed, for his conscientious stand against Henry VIII's ecclesiastical policy. In this, he is very alone. Actual letters of his to his daughter Meg convey his state of mind: he could see former colleagues chatting merrily as they sauntered to the buttery, and one can almost hear Thomas saying, 'How can it be so easy for them?' or 'Why must it be so difficult for me?' In the play, Thomas is visited by his sturdy, uncomprehending wife, Alice. She has brought some gifts, and Thomas tries to be appreciative:

'You still make superlative custard, Alice.'

'Do I?'

'That's a nice dress you have on . . .'

Alice at this point explodes:

'I know I'm a fool, but I'm no such fool as [. . .] to relish complimenting on my custard . . .'

So starts a tirade in which she tells him what she thinks of his obstinacy. Thomas stops – the tone has become real – and ('just hanging on to his self-possession') he says, 'Alice, if you can tell me that you understand, I think I can make a good death, if I have to . . .'[1]

'If you tell me you understand me, I think I can go through with it.' John of the Cross knows how far the 'going through' can go. It may be hard to credit it, but he writes of a night (presumably his own, presumably in Toledo) where the gentleness of God so exposes a person's inner crudity that he feels 'cast off by God', fit to be 'loathed by everyone and everything' – even by God – 'for ever'.[2] That, and all the physical, emotional, spiritual unhinging that leads up to it, is how much a person may 'go through', and it is important for such a one to be understood.

Jesus wanted, not necessarily to dismiss pain, but to sustain faith in the pain; so John is aware that one can go through with it, not if suffering is lessened to my threshold, but if I know I am not alone.

There is the problem. Ultimately, we do not want to base our journey just on the wisdom of some sixteenth-century Spaniard. Only Jesus could make John's teaching universal. 'There is no other name under heaven given among men by which we must be saved' than that of Jesus (Acts 4:12). Yet when one picks up the Spaniard's works, they seem disconcertingly thin on Jesus's name. Worse, the books of the *Night* are particularly thin on it, where, if anywhere, the companionship of Christ would seem to be important.

Some authors have asked just how Christian John of the Cross was. The theologian Karl Rahner, generally favourable towards him, suggests that the friar had secondarily to correct a 'start on a pantheistic basis'.[3] We can make the point with a somewhat unfair statistic: the word 'Jesús' occurs in John's longer works (700 pages of Spanish edition) only four times. Admittedly '*Jesucristo*' occurs as much again, and '*Cristo*' and '*Hijo*' (Son) are frequent enough. But the problem is there.

John's picture of human degradation recorded in the night is really a question about the Incarnation. One response to inner city deprivation is that people of prayer should go and live in deprived areas and be a presence there, because – in this view – part of Incarnation is just 'being with'. Well, is it? If it is, how far is it? Is God a masterful physician who diagnoses from afar? Or is he someone who has gone to the scene of disease or famine and attended close hand? Or is he someone who, when he attends, really knows what he is doing because he has first caught the disease and starved from the hunger?

This question has to be put to John because he has sounded the depth of human suffering as few others. For John, does Incarnation mean that the Son of God has been precisely there, and suffered it; or is night a place which the Son of God has cured, but to which he has never gone? Are people who are experiencing a nightlike obscurity going to be merely tended by the heavenly physician, or does he, first, from the inside, understand them?

To answer the question from John's point of view, we need to get on to his wavelength. We shall look at that first.

## How to read St John of the Cross

'I can see that Christ is very little known by those who think themselves his friends.'[5] This startling statement of John's suggests that, when he talks about Christ, he is not going to say just what everybody else says. If, in his writing as a whole, John's intention is not to repeat, but to deepen, not to add more bits, but to enable a genuine benefiting from the bits we already have, this is especially true when we look at the place of Jesus. It is a test case in reading John's works correctly.

First, John's word about Christ does a specific job. His aim is not to expound credal statements about Jesus; or develop a series of meditations on, say, the Passion; or exhort people to service on the model of Jesus's service – though all of these were prevalent in his day. He is going to tell us Christ's place in the vital movement upon which all those other approaches depend: the God who is giving himself, and the space in the person for that gift. That was the pattern of John's experience: '*todo*', 'everything', the gift; and '*nada*', 'nothing', the space. It is Christ's vital involvement in this that we need, on coming to terms with John, to know.

That means, secondly, that there will be matters important to John in his life that are not treated in his works; so that a knowledge of his life is particularly helpful in the case of this author. The fact is that Hispanic Christmas dramas, Eucharistic processions, drawings of the Crucified, songs about the Good Shepherd, gave colour to John's year and to the life of his communities.

'Among the mysteries he loved most were, it seemed to me, the mystery of the Most Holy Trinity, and also the Son of God made human (*humanado*).' That was the observation of one Sister Maria.[6] Others say John would become enthusiastic when he talked about the Virgin Mary or about the Eucharist.[7] Either way, the human Jesus – Son made flesh, mother of the flesh, sacramental flesh – seems in life to have been a preferred topic.

His letters confirm it. St Teresa's tend to begin, 'The Holy Spirit be in your Reverence . . .' John chose a different opening: 'Jesus be in your soul'. Though the word 'Jesus' may not cram the concordance of the author's longer writings, when it comes to correspondence with people dear to him, what he wants for them is that the human 'Jesus' be 'in' them.

There is a touching letter of his to the nun, Ana de San Alberto.[8]

She and John were the same age, and they were close enough to be frank. The letter lets us in on John's prayer: he asks Ana, when she feels the need of support, to go to Christ, because that is where he goes – to 'that spotless mirror of the Eternal Father' – and he sees her there every day.

If Jesus so filled John's daily life, his presence should be perceptible in the writings. It is, so long as we switch over to John's linguistic atmosphere. This is a third criterion for reading John: learn his language. '*Jesús*', '*Jesucristo*' are rare. 'Christ', 'Word', 'Son', 'Lord' are more common. But characteristic are more personal or poetic ways of speaking about Christ. 'Bridegroom' and 'Beloved' primarily refer to him, and together they occur about 550 times.

The vocabulary becomes quite psychedelic. We might be hard put to remember when we last referred to Christ with one of these terms: Brother, shepherd, health, ransom, medicine, mountain goat, stag, lion, garden, fountain, rock, deep mine, well of Bethlehem, lily of the valleys, light of the eyes, prisoner, sweet nightingale! When one learns John's idiom, Jesus's presence spreads rapidly.

Fourth, John sometimes writes passing phrases – tips of icebergs – which show the way he is thinking but which do not get developed. For instance, the Bridegroom in *Canticle* – the object of the whole search and the One really searching – is identified at the very end as 'the most sweet Jesus, the Bridegroom of faithful souls . . .'[9] The power unleashed on John of the Cross in the *Living Flame* is identified as the vitality of the risen Christ – 'I live, now not I, but Christ lives in me.'[10] The letting-go discussed in *Ascent* has one motive and model: 'love for Jesus Christ' whose only food was 'doing the will of his Father'.[11] The one who enters the space of the purified soul in the same work is named as the 'Son of God'.[12] And the desperate longing which fuels the pain of night is disclosed as a need for the Easter Jesus, on the model of Mary Magdalene anxious at the sepulchre.[13]

A last criterion: it is important in reading John not to be beguiled by quantity. Whereas Teresa will tell you what is important to her and repeat it till there is no mistaking her, John may say what is important to him once; in the wrong place. Sometimes there are signposts which say, this is a hinge chapter – the rest of the book depends on it.[14] That is so of *Ascent* book two, chapter five, which tells us that the goal of this whole process is, not just perfection, but union – relationship, with God. It is true too of key statements about Jesus (we shall come to them). They do not take up many pages, but without them the book loses its consistency – they are really its spine.

These then are criteria for reading John, which are specially helpful in understanding the place of Jesus in his writings:

- relate the question to the central pattern: gift, space for the gift;
- be aware of John's life and pastoral ministry;
- tune into the special atmosphere and language;
- look out for passing phrases which tell you how the author is thinking;
- take hinge paragraphs or chapters seriously.

With the help of these tools, it is worth now getting to grips with John's understanding of Jesus. If his work as a whole emerges from his experience, and if we came to understand his main thrust (gift, *todo*; space, *nada*) by going back to that, presumably we will best understand John's view of Jesus by following the same route. In the next chapter we shall search for Jesus in the pattern of the works as a whole. But here we want to root that in the Toledo experience which generated all that John later has to say.

## Who is Jesus for John of the Cross?

A way to begin might be to ask this: suppose someone approached you, someone who had been instructed in the Christian faith, but who is searching for its meaning in their life. The person says to you, 'I was brought up a Christian, and I know about the Bible, but I want to find out: what does Jesus mean for *you*?' In answering that, what phrase, or image, or memory would come to mind?

That was John's question in Toledo. He had learned about Jesus as a child, read Scripture carefully, examined the issues at university. He had preached Christ and guided others towards him. But now, beyond anything he had experienced before, he needed to meet him; Jesus, whom he had always known, but, it now seemed, had never really known. His prison canticle put it neatly: 'Where have you hidden, Beloved?'

'What does Jesus mean for me?' That was the real drama of John's imprisonment; and, thankfully, he shares with us his answer.

The answer comes in a poem we have scarcely mentioned, but which forms the prologue to all the works – the lenses through which they all have to be viewed. It is the *Romances* or *Ballads* on the Incarnation: John's reflection, in faith, on the mystery of Christmas. The *Ballads* are his statement, then, of who Jesus is for him, when he needs an answer.

John was jailed early in December. The *Ballads* have a strong Advent tone. They could well have been the first verses he composed in his dungeon. Unlike his other major poems – *Flame*, *Canticle*, *Night*, *Fountain* – these are not an obvious fruit of poetic genius. They are basic, rustic. Ballads were a common form: popular songs, with easy rhymes and rhythm, usually telling a love story – the kind of thing John's older brother got into trouble for singing with the lads round the streets of Arévalo.

In the Golden Age of sixteenth-century Spain, setting Christian themes to popular tunes was nothing new: saintly evangelists were keen on the technique, men like John of God, servant of the sick, or the Franciscans Peter of Alcántara and Paschal Baylon. The enlightened bishop of Granada, Hernando de Talavera, even wrote Christian songs in Arabic for his Moorish population. In particular, Teresa's reform of the Carmelite Order relished an atmosphere of family cheer. *La Madre* composed her own Christmas repertoire; and several of her sisters produced, specifically, 'ballads'. Teresa had been careful to initiate her new recruit, Fray John, into the light touch and tuneful feel of her communities. She writes of how she brought him to experience 'the way we live as sisters together and the kind of recreation we take'. Teresian reform included, for John, Teresian festivity, and *Ballads* came naturally to him.[15]

At a time of trauma, one might think back to a song or carol one learned as a child, and sing it as a way of keeping sane. It would be simple, but it would say what needed to be said. So with John here. Easy songs, popular metre, Teresian cheer, Christmas: he resorted to the form that came easiest, to express his faith in what was most homely, in circumstances that were, for him, most alienating.

That is the scene: a young man, flogged, starved and left in a dark hole, accused by the very walls of failure, guilt, rejection; fit to be 'loathed by everything', to be 'loathed and rejected by God – quite rightly – for ever'.[16] What did he find to say into that?

The *Ballads* comprise nine scenes. Though the rhyme may be unspectacular, the theology they contain is astounding, the more so for being so neatly compressed.

The first three scenes set us in a universe of generosity: the Trinity. Far from being tame or flat ('It's Trinity Sunday – it'll be a short sermon'), John finds there irrepressible energy. He portrays a Father and Son who are, simply, amazed at each other, 'gone', gone out to each other. There is a kind of rhapsody in the Father's admission, 'nothing gives me joy, Son, / outside of your company . . .' They are 'lover and beloved' who 'live' in each other, and whose shared vitality is the Holy Spirit.[17]

The Trinity appears here as act, event, where the Father is always conceiving the Son, the Son is always reinvesting love in the Father. Theirs is not a stale or level love; it escalates up and out the more intensive it is: 'love, the more it is one, / the greater the love it bestows.'[18]

Already we have a lesson here. Poverty and bestowal are the co-ordinates of John's system not merely because that is how things have to be for us as human beings. Things are that way because that is how God is: Father, Son and Spirit are each absolutely poor because they each give themselves completely – so each is utterly rich with the other's generosity. 'So the Son's glory, / is the glory he has in the Father; / and all the Father's glory / he possesses in the Son.'[19]

The rapture and surprise in the love of each person for the other comes out in the third scene, where Father and Son discuss the project of creation. 'A bride who might love you, / my Son . . .'[20] The Father wants to share his appreciation of his Son. The Son thinks that is a wonderful idea – 'thank you very much, Father . . .'[21] – because the bride can then relish the beauty of the Father. Father wants bride to enjoy Son; Son wants bride to relish Father. It is as if creation were the fruit of an excess of unselfishness.

A word of command – 'Let it be done'[22] – and the universe is created. This starts the fourth *Ballad*. It is here that the Son's plan, and the poet's understanding of who Jesus is, takes shape.

The plan matches the arclike movement of the Word in the Fourth Gospel – 'I came from the Father and have come into the world; again, I am leaving the world and going to the Father' (John 16:28). So here the Son intends a cosmic sweep in which he will embrace his bride, 'tenderly [. . .] give her his love', and lift her into the life of the Father.[23] Where the bride, the 'body' of which

Christ is the 'head', is meant as humankind, the rescue will involve sacrifice:

> 'for in all things like to them / he would himself become / and he would come to them / and with them make his home, / and God would be man / and man would God become / he would spend with them his time / and eat and drink together / and with them he would stay, / he himself in constancy.'[24]

If this is who Jesus is for John, what is the emphasis?

Without forcing anything, there is a stress on being with. Being with, in all our mundanity: eating, drinking, staying, spending time. When a person is with another, something is taking place – something potentially enormous. When the Son is with mankind, he is not just 'there'. An exchange of energy takes place, with huge consequences: 'God would be man, and man would God become'.

When Thomas Aquinas asks the reason for the Incarnation, he says magnificent and very helpful things. But ultimately he considers that the Word would not have become flesh had there been no sin for which to atone.[25]

In John's theological studies, this question of Aquinas's was on the curriculum. Yet here in the *Ballads*, written a decade after John's university days, sin is not the prominent issue. Now, when John has been taken beyond his own threshold, it is important not only that the Son should forgive, but that he should stay with, be with.

The *Ballads* continue (scene five) with a medley of Old Testament quotations summing up the bride's Advent longing – 'Oh that you would tear the heavens open and come down . . .'[26] Longing means 'agony', 'tears', 'groans'; it is longing for the Son's *compañía*, companionship.[27] This accumulated desire banks up in the old man, Simeon (*Ballad* six), who, in hope, waits.

Then *Ballad* seven: on the threshold of the Incarnation, another scene-shift introduces a touching dialogue between Father and Son. It is as if the Father, now that the moment has come, were anxious to coax his Son into what, he knows, will be cruelly painful. Father says 'with tender love', 'You see, Son . . .'[28] The speech goes like this: You see, Son, that your bride has been made in your image, and insofar as she is like you, she suits you very well. But she is different in that she has flesh . . . Perfect love has a law, that the lover should want to be like the one he loves . . .

The Son hops over the Father's tact with an irrepressible 'Yes!' His Father's will is his total delight; and the chance which it gives him of announcing to the world his Father's 'beauty', 'gentleness' and 'sovereignty', is for him irresistible.[29]

We shall come back to the Son's closing words in *Ballad* seven; but in the following scene the tone turns homely as we enter the dwelling of a young Galilean woman. There will be a wonderful exchange, if Mary will allow it . . . She will: she surrenders to the Word, and the wedding of the Bridegroom–Son and the Bride–humankind takes place. But there is a touch of dissonance in the closing scene (*Ballad* nine). While the wedding celebration goes on around (angels, shepherds), Mary gazes at her crying baby. She is stunned at what the exchange is meaning: while man is getting to know joy, God is discovering tears.

Back to the response to the Father's coaxing (*Ballad* seven). The Son is eagerly saying 'Yes' to his Father's design. His enthusiasm reaches a climax with the words:

'I shall go to seek my bride / and I myself shall shoulder / her weariness and troubles / in which she suffers so / and, that life might now be hers / for her I will to die, / and drawing her from the lake / to you I shall restore her.'[30]

If this is who Jesus is for John, what is the emphasis here? Things have moved a stage further. The emphasis is on 'being with', 'company', but company that shares pain. The Son wants to 'be with' from the inside, from inside her weariness and troubles in which she suffers so.

In order to rescue the bride from 'the lake', the Son wills first to drown with her in the lake.

That is who Jesus is for John of the Cross, as he begins months of isolation and bitter disapproval, when everything – his body, his friends, his future, his sense of purpose, even the God of his fathers – turns stranger. In faith, Jesus is the one whom John encounters at his side, weeping his tears and feeling his anguish, sweetening what is immeasurably bitter by his spousal love.

When John later writes about gift and space, night and flame, he writes it out of that.

# 18: Jesus, the Experience of God

John's word – an inflowing God, space for the gift – emerged from his experience; and Toledo was the furnace which fired that experience. The question about the importance, or lack of it, of Jesus for John has to be answered there. In his *Ballads*, he has answered it for us there. When he needed to say something – not to teach, or direct, or comment, but just because he needed to say it (the witnesses say that is why he wrote poetry) – what he said was 'Jesus', who filled John in a poverty he had first shared.

If that is where John's view of Jesus starts, we are in place now to follow it through in his major writings – along those two lines: where is Jesus in the doctrine on God's self-gift; and where is he in the doctrine on making room? First, God's gift, the *todo*, the 'all', which gives the *nada* any meaning.

We can focus here on two hinge chapters: one in *Ascent*, the work stressing the need to rely on God, in faith, and not on other supports; and one in *Canticle*, which presents the whole drama as a journey.

First, *Ascent*. When John says, 'Not this, nor that, nor that, but faith', it can bring a marvellous sense of spaciousness and freedom; but it can also bring a feeling of rootlessness. It is all very well his telling us to let go of secondary supports, but we have to hold on to *something*. The books of the *Ascent* revolve around this 'something', and it takes a hinge chapter to name it (unlucky for those who don't read that far, but that is John's style!). The hinge is *Ascent*, book two, chapter 22. The author holds up a clear signpost announcing its centrality: 'to clarify our subject and establish its doctrinal foundation . . .'[1] The chapter makes great reading on its own. But when it is put in context, it becomes very powerful.

To put it in context, a race through the twenty-one chapters that go before: 1–4, faith is a meeting, with God, in darkness; 5, the goal is union; 6, theological virtue brings you there; (7 we shall hop over); 8, feelings and concepts cannot actually deliver God in himself; 9, faith can and does; then come the alternatives to faith (listed in 10); 12–15, thinking about and imagining gospel scenes is important, but the time may come to go beyond pictures for the sake of more total presence; as for experiencing extraordinary phenomena, like apparitions (11, 16), this should not be actively sought – they do not give you God in himself; 17, God sometimes bestows these experiences because of a person's concrete needs, but, 18, they can still be misunderstood – 19, Scripture shows us that; 20, even biblical personages could take up divine communications wrongly; and just because, 21, God answers when people ask for a sign, it does not mean he is pleased with that request. And so we come to 22. If, in the Old Covenant, people did ask for signs and were right to rely on extraordinary phenomena – prophets, dreams, priestly divination – why can we not cling to supernatural signs and experiences now?

The whole of the book rises to this question: What should we seek, if we don't seek all of that? Put otherwise, the author says: not this, nor that, nor that, nor this, nor – and we say, 'Well, what?! We have to look somewhere!' Again, John says, faith, faith, faith, faith – and we say, 'What *is* this faith for which we sacrifice everything else?'

The answer: Jesus Christ.

'In giving us, as he did, his Son, who is his only Word – he has no other – he has spoken it all to us, once and for all, in this only Word; he has no more to say.'[2]

Faith, to which all other means should be subordinated, now receives definition: Christ is the only 'proximate means to union with God'.[3] He is the 'somewhere' to which we must uniquely look. He is the Gift for which space must urgently be made.

This is the meaning of the '*nada*, nothing': a space shaped for Christ. In *Flame* John showed how any emptiness is because of a greater fullness: there, to the bride-soul, 'all things are nothing; she is in her own eyes nothing. Only her God is, for her, everything (*todo*)'.[4] Now the everything receives a name:

'God has become mute and has no more to say: what he used to say partially, to the prophets, he has now said totally, in his Son, giving us his Son, who is our Everything . . .'[5]

If he is everything, he contains in himself the good that is in anything else. Religious experiences, charismatic gifts, supernatural phenomena, insights and uplifts – these are all excellent, if they point to Christ; they can be real motives for love, if they do not glue us to themselves but impel us to Christ, his word, his community.[6] Otherwise, they will prove a (perhaps wonderful) irrelevance.

For John this was not cold doctrine: it kept his hope alive and was the source of his joy. In his prayer, he knew his own 'meanness and limitations'; but 'You will not take from me my God, what you once gave me in your only Son Jesus Christ, in whom you gave me *all* I long for; so I shall rejoice: you will not delay, if I do not fail to hope.'[7]

That is the gift: not just what Jesus said, but who he personally is: the Word, who reveals by being given, and who speaks by being.

This is the *risen* Christ, spoken once into history, and now eternally alive. He is the event of faith who 'gives us an experience of God'. Risen – available, impinging, pressing to come in, held out to us as given. So for 'anyone who wanted to question God' or who sought to receive 'some vision or revelation', the Father would present this manifesto:

'If I have already said all things to you in my Word, my Son, and if I have no other, what kind of answer could I give you now, or what could I reveal that would surpass this? Set your eyes on him alone, because in him I have said it all to you [. . .] and you will find in him even more than you are asking, more even than you desire. [. . .] He is my total locution and vision, my total revelation and the whole of my reply. This I have already spoken to you, [. . .] *giving* him to you as Brother, Companion, Master, Ransom and Reward.'[8]

In *Canticle* there is a different atmosphere. The darkness there is more of the heart than the mind, where the bride, for all her clarity, feels rootless, homeless, until the Other is at her centre. The search is in the key of love, with its own kind of gift and its own way of receiving. The gift is 'Christ, the Bridegroom'. If she keeps 'turning over and handling these mysteries [. . .] of faith, she will deserve that love disclose what faith contains: the Bridegroom'.⁹

The point is that love takes the person on a journey deeper into him. Deeper, but always into him. *Canticle* brings waves of understanding, unveiling each time what was there from the beginning. It is as if one heard a drama on the radio about children being saved from drowning; then it turns out to be a news item, not a drama; then one discovers the children are one's own children.

So, the bride's search starts off with a meditation on the mysteries of Jesus – meaning Jesus born, tempted, teaching, healing, praying, sweating, dying, rising. She begins with this. As she goes further, she comes . . . to the mysteries of Jesus; surpassing that she reaches . . . the mysteries of Jesus; until finally, in the utter newness of heaven, she will be overwhelmed by the mysteries of Jesus.

What began, then, as wholesome piety (*1A* 13), develops into a raging sore (*CB* 7) – Give me no more messages: 'You be the messenger and the message!'¹⁰ What was felt as a sore, becomes a healing (*CB* 22). She had been involved all along in the life of the Healer (*CB* 23). The layers keep unfolding, until finally the Healer becomes her home, his mysteries the living space in which both can be alive (*CB* 37). She, and he, enter the caverns, *las cavernas*, which are himself.

> And so up to the caverns,
> set deep into the rock
> – almost out of sight –
> we'll find a way to enter,
> there to taste the pomegranate wine (*Canticle* stanza 32).

'O my dove, in the clefts of the rock . . .' (Song of Songs 2:14). Using Solomon's language, John's stanza reflects for him the union for which he has been striving, and anticipates the fullness of heaven. The commentary is a pivotal chapter.

The caverns, the living space, are the mysteries of Jesus.¹¹ Entering means taking on the shape of Jesus' life so as to meet Jesus's heart.

> 'The soul longs really to enter these caverns, Christ's caverns, so that she might indeed be absorbed, transformed, drunk with

the love their wisdom contains, hiding herself in the heart of her Beloved.'[12]

The caverns remain even in heaven: the risen Christ is what he is now, because of all he went through then. All he experienced then is alive in him. His earthliness is risen; but being risen, its vitality is infinite. John has emphasised the otherness of God. The journey into the heart of Christ which *Canticle* traces does not compromise that. In Christ, God's otherness is communicated, not dissolved. For John, Christ is himself the receding depth which makes the divine 'always new and increasingly amazing'.[13]

'However much saintly teachers have discovered and holy people understood [. . .] the greater part remains to be said, and even to be understood. There is much to fathom in Christ. He is like a huge mine with seam after seam of treasures. However deeply you dig, never will you find an end or come to a conclusion . . .'[14]

John does say that the time may come, in prayer, when it will be unhelpful to spend energy picturing gospel scenes.[15] That is fair enough: what we want is the person, not pictures of the person. But there is nothing secondary about the role of Christ. John knows him, not as a potential hindrance, but as the universe's open sluice-gate to the divine. He is the only place from which one can gaze on the Father unrestrictedly: 'thanking the Father and loving him anew with great delight and feeling, through his Son Jesus Christ. And this she does united with Christ, together with Christ.'[16]

Heaven will be that: a total entry into the caverns of Christ's heart, an infinite space for the Father.

That accounts for Jesus' place in half of the dynamic: the gift, the All, faith as presence. Unequivocally, John names it as the Son of God risen in his flesh. Jesus *is* that half of the dynamic.

What about the other half: the space, *nada*, faith as darkness? There is a hint back in 2 *Ascent* 22: part of the Father's manifesto there runs like this:

'If you want me to answer with some word of comfort, look at my Son, subject to me and subjected, afflicted, out of love for me – and you will see how many words of comfort he will speak to you.'[17]

When the Son speaks comfort, he speaks it with the strength of experience. His gift is, first, his companionship. Another hinge chapter (the one we hopped over in the summary of Book Two of *Ascent*) drives this implacably home.

As it becomes clear that John's programme can lead not just to upright behaviour, but to inner poverty and total emptiness, it is hardly surprising that we may feel misgivings. That is where John's hinge chapter, 2 *Ascent* 7, aims to meet us.

He does need to meet us. He needs to ground his invitation to go forward on sometimes naked faith, and on a love that can lead one to die for the other. That is the active side; but more than that, all he has to say about the obscurity that can submerge one's horizons, till it fogs out the lighting of the soul, that, especially, needs justifying.

The undergirding has to address the whole programme, not just part of the programme. The hinge chapter comes in *Ascent*, the work ostensibly about the active side of our journey. It is *Night* that focuses on the passive side, on the darkness that comes upon us and can empty out one's inmost spirit. But, in the mind of the author, *Ascent* and *Night* are two halves of a single project, in which he shows that the night which comes upon us is his real concern. He looks towards that from the start,[18] and when he has dealt with that, he feels that 'the main reason for my setting to work' has been addressed.[19] When, in the chapter we are looking at now, he takes time out to underpin his message, the whole message, especially 'the main' message, is in view.

John reasons like this: I know that what I am saying seems to be stretching things, so I want to show that it comes, not from me, but from Christ.[20]

He begins with Jesus's words. The call to discipleship means a narrow gate and a tight passage; it means denying self, taking a cross, and following. Here, losing life is gaining; it is cup, sweet yoke, entry to the sheepfold.[21] When a person goes forward without pay-offs, in darkness, dryness, to please God, that is 'the cross, pure and spiritual, nakedness of spirit, the poverty of Christ'.[22]

What John has to say, then, he believes to be thoroughly

unoriginal. It is lifted straight from the gospel. Still, words are not enough. It is not enough for Jesus to have said, 'night'; it is important in John's view that he should also have experienced it, since 'he is our example and our light'.[23]

This introduces the great statement. As we said, it has to be strong enough to carry all the weight of pain that John is going to plumb in succeeding chapters. That means not just the struggle of effort ('active'), but the reversal that comes upon us ('passive'); not only at the level of physical hardship or pain ('sense'), but at the more inward level that shakes or stifles me as a person ('spirit'). There has to be a home here for the person who has come to feel 'abandoned' by God, fit to be 'loathed by everyone and everything' – even by God – 'for ever'.[24] John's logic here is almost too daring. It is worth reading the passage gently:

'. . . progress lies only in imitating Christ: he is the way and the truth and the life, and no one comes to the Father but by him . . . So any person who wanted to go forward in sweetness and ease and ran from imitating Christ, well, I would not be happy about it.

Since I have said that Christ is the way, and that this way means dying to our natural selves in sense and spirit, I would like to show how this is modelled on Christ, since he is our example and light.

First of all [referring then to sense], there is no doubt that Christ died to sense – spiritually, during his life; and naturally, at his death. For, as he said himself, in his life he had nowhere to lay his head; and at his death, he had less.

Second, [so, the level of spirit] it is certain that at the moment of death he was also annihilated in soul, without any comfort or relief; the Father left him that way in innermost dryness, according to the lower part. That is why he was compelled to cry out, 'My God! My God! Why have you forsaken me?' This was the most extreme feeling of forsakenness he had had in his life. And by it he did his greatest work – greater than any he had done in his life, however miraculous, on earth or in heaven. That is, he reconciled and united the human race with God through grace.

This he did, as I say, at the time, the very moment when this Lord was most annihilated in all things: in his human reputation, since in seeing him die people mocked him instead of in any way valuing him; in his natural self, since there he was annihilated in dying; and in support and in spiritual comfort from the Father, since at that time he deserted him, so that he might pay the debt without qualification and might unite humankind with God – staying like that, annihilated, and reduced as to nothing.'[25]

For John, the experience of God's love is truest when it is too deep for words.[26] In a related way, his picture of Christ's love – annihilated, contorted, deserted – is too deep for comment.

What follows, then, is footnote rather than explanation.

It is vital not to minimalise the scope of what John says here, because it is one of Christianity's greatest appreciations of the death of its Lord, and to short-change it would be to take away from believers something they may one day, in their own pain, need desperately to hear.

It has been suggested that John stops short of associating Jesus with the night of the spirit. The inclusion of the phrases, 'according to the lower part', and 'feeling of' in the fourth paragraph are seen as John's way of drawing back from that association.

This is incorrect. The whole point of the chapter is to prepare the reader to accept whatever will come in the rest of the work. If Jesus were being proposed as a model only of more peripheral pain (for all its terror), that would make the chapter pointless. 'You can go there because Christ has been there'; that is John's logic.

What is more, Jesus is *especially* associated with that inner pain which bites at the level of spirit: 'annihilated in soul', 'innermost dryness', no 'spiritual' comfort. And despite the location of the passage in a book (II *Ascent*) ostensibly about the 'active night' (what we do), Jesus's night was all about what happened to him – the more penetrating 'passive night'. Jesus knew the night where what should not be, is.

John, like Aquinas, does talk about Jesus's physical pain and his loss of reputation. But John is determined to follow through the consequences of the Cross. For him, the real focus is in Jesus's relationship with his Father. That is where he feels abandoned. Jesus retrieves the sinner, the human race of sinners, by walking the sinner's distance from the Father and retrieving him *there*.

Why, then, the phrases 'lower part' and 'feeling of'?

We are capable of knowing at one level and not knowing at another: there is the knowledge of words, of images, of concept, of feeling, of presence. A person can know their name, but not be thinking of their name. Someone in love can be concentrating on question four of their mathematics exam, and still know they are in love. This is all obvious enough. But the layering of the human spirit seems to go further. A person can know God more and be able to talk about God less. The saints can know hellish darkness and still speak of a kind of peace – but still be going through hellish darkness. The mystics are familiar with depths of spirit which have their own mode of knowing, untranslatable on to more customary levels.

It is human, then, to know and not to know at the same time. So, presumably, with the Son-made-human, Jesus, whose spirit is an unfathomable mine. To speak of 'lower' allows there still to be a 'higher', an even deeper.[27] So John's phrases, 'lower part', 'feeling', are his way of allowing, through traditional terminology, that the crucified Jesus, annihilated at all the levels with which we are familiar, was still, at a level deeper or higher than his thinking mind and feeling heart, at the fine-point of his .spirit, uniquely in communion with his Father. The annihilation of the cross as it were scraped off every other layer to let that layer pulsate unrestrainedly. On the cross, the heart of Jesus became a massive space for the fire of the Spirit to burn – free to blaze out, 'more intense than all the fires in the world,'[28] in resurrection.

Something else worth noting: the words 'most extreme forsakenness – greatest work – greater than any other he had done' ring a bell. They follow the same pattern as John's statement about the primacy of love. 'A little of this pure love is more precious to God . . . and of more benefit to the Church, even though it seems to be doing nothing, than all those other works put together.'[29] John learned that from Jesus. And Jesus taught him the nature of that love. That 'pure love' may bring radiant elation. On the other hand it may feel as rough as a splintered cross-beam. It may come as dryness, darkness, the over-exacting demand not to renege on one's integrity. If it does, John says, know that you are not alone, and that you are helping to save the world.

John ends the passage by making that connection:

'This is so that the really spiritual person might understand [. . .] that the more annihilated she be for God [. . .] the more is she united with God, and the greater the work she does.

It doesn't consist, then, in good times or sweet spiritual feelings, but in a living, sensory and spiritual, exterior and interior, death on the cross.'[30]

Why does John say that in *Ascent*, but not in the book where he describes the spirit's stripping, the *Night*? On careful reading, Jesus is present in *Night*: it is love for him that empowers the person's search;[31] union with him, the 'Son of God', is the goal that makes it all worth while;[32] and the 'immense love of Christ the Word', the risen Christ who kept the disciples' hope alive, appears, furtively, at points in the drama.[33] Jesus is present at the start and the close, and odd moments in between. But for most of the book, he does not appear.

That ties in with the main point of the book *Night*. The book means to tell us, not so much what is actually happening in the night of spirit, but how it feels. John wants to prepare us for night by simulating its crude obscurity as much as literature can. What night *feels* is 'senseless'. 'If I knew God was in it, I could go through with it', but the point is that God feels not to be in it. That is what makes it night. John wants us to be prepared for that, and, in that, not to panic.

Godless is how it feels. Actually, the darkness of spirit which John plumbs is divine light too close to focus, love felt as pain.

That said, the face of Christ is not so far from the *Night* picture as at first seems. He is there, but there from the inside. The journey is not any journey. It is a way of the 'cross'.[34] It is hanging in mid-air, unable to breathe.[35] It is the belly of the whale, the belly of the earth, the 'sepulchre of dark death', prelude to 'the resurrection'.[36]

In the night, Jesus is not only 'there'. His dying and rising is an active force, prone, if allowed, to unfold its compacted meaning. He shapes us from within. The *nada* is *his* emptiness. The darkness that can eat into human life, with its threat of isolation and appearance of chaos, has taken on Christ's contours. It has become a space for his Father to fill.

'Jesus' is far from secondary to this sixteenth-century Spaniard. But he does view him in a particular light, and this has its consequences. He dares to propose him as model in the night, at its worst – the terrible night, *horrenda noche*. The texts mean that, whatever the person may be suffering, Jesus has touched and sanctified that abyss. Jesus may not have shared the pain in kind – he did not know what it was to grow old, to lose a child, or to sin. But he has searched out every pain in intensity. The suffering of the Son of God, wrecked, mocked, deserted and Godforsaken, offers a home for everyone's sorrow.

John's vision, then, has consequences. It means that I am never alone; wherever I may have to go, Jesus has been there, Jesus is there. John's Christ is the understanding Christ, the Christ who knows what it is like to be me.

However, if Christ's companionship is that far-reaching, and his love is that dynamic, John's vision commits believers, not simply to acknowledging formulae about Jesus, or to following a benign ethic; it commits them to allowing Jesus to work out his dying and rising in their lives.

# 19: Prayer: Should we? Can we?

Something is taking place, and it is important to be part of it. That is the intuition which John of the Cross has been communicating. It comes across in the whole pattern he has traced – an approaching God, who gives where he finds space, and who works in darkness to create that space. It is there when the pattern concentrates into the here and now – faith, hope, love, our yes to God's gift of himself. Now the happening has received the name 'Jesus' – who has searched out our darkness, and is himself the gift.

This is taking place, and it is important to be part of it. For John, becoming part of it is prayer.

In fact, this master in prayer uses the word 'prayer' sparingly. It could connote merely something that one does, at a particular time, in a specific way. When this is what is implied, energy goes into finding a way of praying, describing a method; and, while John does consider this worth while, it is not the primary question.

More important for him, of more practical importance, are the questions: does prayer have value – now, for me? and is prayer a possibility – now, for me? What can make prayer difficult is the feeling that it is not really feeding me; or the unspoken fear that, even if I say the right things and am diligent and faithful, prayer – as a living encounter with the radiant God – will always elude me.

Our inventiveness would surely stretch to finding a method, if we were given assurance about those more fundamental questions: is prayer really what I need? is the prayer I want a real possibility?

John's witness has been a large-scale answer to these questions. As the lines he has traced now converge around prayer, it will be good to re-express his answer, then to draw from it the help he offers when we come to the what and the how.

## Prayer: a supreme value

John of the Cross had prayed long, and expertly guided others
in their own prayer journey. But we saw that, when he finally
gave expression to his relationship with God, the first word was
a bewildered cry exposing a raw wound – a world outside John's
control where the only certainty was his hunger.

> Where have you hidden,
> Beloved, and left me groaning?
> You fled like a stag
> having wounded me;
> I went out in search of you, and you were gone
> (Canticle stanza 1).

'Where are you . . .?' Chronologically, John's mature writing
career began here. But, more than that, this first stanza of his
prison *Canticle* discloses his constant motivation. 'Where . . .? . . .
I went out': it was his hunger that fed his search and made him live
the way he did. At the centre of John's story is his need.

Prayer meant getting in touch with that need. And the friar
did touch it not only in dramatic crises (as in Toledo), but in
more routine circumstances. Simply, when John had a problem,
he asked God.

Eliseus, one of the most eloquent witnesses to his character,
gives us an insight into this. John's 'need', in the cases Eliseus
describes, was for a cool head when others' blood-pressures were
running high. We are told first something about John's vision of
authority:

> 'He told me once that if we see courtesy die in the Order . . .
> and in its place superiors who are rough and aggressive – and
> that is a vice proper to barbarians – then we should weep for the
> Order: it would be lost. Since when have people been beaten
> into loving virtue, or encouraged in the way of God by harsh
> treatment?'

This is part of John's characteristic sensitivity to the individual.
But he apparently linked it with courage to speak out in public –
otherwise the little ones get crushed. This happens when those in
authority keep 'their mouth shut and accept whatever is proposed,

just because they are looking after their own corner. This all does serious harm to the common good, and ambition takes hold – nobody has spoken up . . .'

Sensitivity to the individual, then, is prepared to confront those who ride roughshod. What gave John insight and courage to follow through such a difficult coupling of qualities? Eliseus goes on: 'whenever he said such things, it was after having spent a long time in *prayer* and *conversation with our Lord*'.[1]

Prayer, conversation with his Lord, was for John a practical recourse: it was where things became clear, where he recovered focus and strength.

He holds out the same recourse to people clutching at extraordinary experiences. In the place of horoscopes and mediums, he would have this alternative:

'In all our needs, struggles and difficulties, we shall find no better, no surer way forward than *prayer* and the hope that God will provide in the way *he* desires . . . When means fail us and we see no way of dealing with our difficulties, it only remains for us to lift our eyes to You, so that *You* might provide as You see best.'[2]

For us too, then, his advice is basic: 'ask God'. But ask in faith: asking, not incidentally, or as a last resort, but as one's principal resort – suspending one's life upon belief in God's involvement.

Do that, because in any prayer, one's whole life is ultimately the issue. One can pray for strength for tomorrow, for forgiveness for the past, for help in the details of today. One can pray for prisoners of conscience, for loved ones and enemies, for the homeless or the rich, for world peace or inner serenity. To pray for each of these is good. But in each case the need, though real, is a symptom of a deeper need, of a craving that is as close and as vital as we are to ourselves. The mystic sounds human needs; and about the person John has said many magnificent things. But the most real thing he says about us is that we are created to *need God* – 'infinite capacity', for God.[3]

Those other needs are symptoms of this universal, most real need, for God. Life can offer signs of it. There is the questioning that remains even when our question has been answered. There is our openness to more love, even when we love and are loved ourselves. There is anxiety. Some coming event – some visit or

undertaking I know I cannot keep putting off – might be a cause
of stress. Yet when it is over, the relief never quite matches the
apprehension one felt before. It is as if this specific anxiety put me
in touch with an inner hole that the specific remedy cannot fill.

So our needs – for answers or love or solutions to our problems
– are symptoms of that greater need, for God. It aches, and its
ache is the price of our dignity. If we are meant for this much,
we shall suffer that hunger.

John designates that dignity by the term 'bride'. In the *Ballads*,
creation was intended to furnish the Son with a 'bride', a whole
people who would be his own.[4] In *Canticle*, the bride is found
and wedded beneath the 'apple tree' of the cross, where 'the Son
of God redeemed, and so betrothed, human nature, and so each
soul, with himself'.[5] This means that humankind, and each person
in it, has, necessarily, a bridal shape. We are, from our origin,
shaped for Christ, a capacity, a need for Christ.

That – our incompleteness – is our dignity, and when we feel
it we are most truly ourselves. When we utter our appeal from
there, we are being mature, being what we were meant to be.
That appeal is prayer. For the human person, then, prayer is a
supreme value.

If prayer lets us become ourselves, it is a supreme value too for
the world. It restores the right rhythm to the universe.

We have already puzzled our way through the statement that
only love saves. John, under the impact of a self-lavishing God,
saw it vital that there should, in the world, be receivers. Only God
saves, and love opens us to a God who does, thankfully, intend to
save. Where the openness is 'pure', God can communicate himself
with unprecedented vigour, like wind roaring through a tunnel. On
this score, people who love keep 'the church' – a world being saved
– alive. John's text read:

> 'A little of this pure love is more precious to God, more precious
> for the soul, and of *more benefit to the Church*, even though
> it seems to be doing nothing, than all those other works put
> together.'[6]

We saw that these words describe Jesus, whose crucified love was
his 'greatest work', opening humankind to God.[7] But now the text
makes an unannounced transition, from 'love' to 'prayer'.

'Those who are very active and think that they are going to
encircle the earth with their preaching . . . should realise that
they would do the Church much more good, and please God
much more . . . if they spent even half of this time *being with
God in prayer* (even though they may not have reached as high
a level as this). In this way they would certainly achieve more,
with less trouble, in one work than they would have done in
a thousand: their prayer would merit it and would give them
inner strength.'8

John's message is forceful: only God saves; crucified love opens
the world to the gift; that love is at work in prayer. Prayer, then,
is an agent of change. Here too, faced with a world in need, John
affirms: prayer is a supreme value.

## Prayer: a real possibility

'How much more will the heavenly Father give *the Holy Spirit* to
those who ask him!' (Luke 11:13) While John is keen to ask for
help, light, solutions – and so, for 'things' – there is really only
one petition, as God has really only one answer. God's answer
is himself, the Spirit of his Son. 'Look at my Son . . . he is my
total reply.'9 If the word 'prayer' is rare, it is giving place to
the language of bride and Bridegroom; of giving and receiving;
of loving and believing; of union. The interest, in prayer, is in
encounter, personal friendship, and John's focus is not on asking
for things, but on being with God.

But there is the fear: is this a real possibility? One senses that,
for the saint, the mystic, of course it is; that, for the person whose
religion is in order and hitch-free, it may well be. But what of
those whose lives are too battered to be pretty, or too busy to
cover all the exits?

John is at least aware of the misgivings. In the prologue to *Ascent*
he says that there are 'many people who think that they do not
pray, and they are praying very much' (though others, he adds,
think they pray superbly, 'and are scarcely praying at all'!).10

John conducted the last years of his ministry in the spangled,
fairy-tale city of Segovia (1588–91). There was nothing magical
though about the disheartening experience of prayer that one
woman, Mariana, was having. She was committed enough, but
she admitted to Fray John that, when she wanted to pray, she

just could not get her thoughts in order. Prayer was, she felt, a waste of time, and she was going to give it up.

The friar understood her. Mariana was an intuitive type, and her way of prayer had to be a loving stillness in simple faith. Apparently she took John's advice. At first, she was aware only of her inner barrenness, but she was told to stay with it. Eventually, we are told, she came to know that stillness as the gentle presence which sustained her life.[11]

The episode is typical of John's vision of prayer. He speaks with security: do not give up. Prayer is possible. It can be actual.

In saying this, he aims to be a realist. We have seen his chapters outlawing the games people play in their piety. But he scrapes off our religious decoration, not because, to his mind, life is grey and the sooner we face that the better ('they're in love now, but it'll soon pass'). He does it instead because he fears we might never connect with the treasure that is within our grasp.

Time and again he sacrifices the superficial – a favourite place, a home-made ritual, a precious feeling – for the sake of something worthy of the sacrifice: *lo vivo* – the living reality, 'substance', 'spirit', 'faith'.

So, John, who loved images (he drew images of Jesus, danced with statues of the infant) is anxious that we pass through, beyond, in search of 'the *living* image within, who is Christ crucified'.[12] John rubbed shoulders with the workmen in Segovia as together they built the friary church; but he warns us not to be mesmerised by bricks-and-mortar beauty – go deeper, 'pray' in 'the living temple' of the soul.[13] There is an unseen vitality at the heart of the human person which guarantees the possibility of prayer.

'The *living* image within, who is Christ crucified.' This is a paschal realism: one which believes in the dying, rising Jesus, as the axis of one's own relationship with God. Dying ('Christ crucified'), as the one who has searched out the unretrieved corners of the human spirit and sat with us there; rising ('the living image within'), as he who, finding us there, folds us into his own life. Faith appears as that: the act of Christ, claiming us from within – as he claimed Mary Magdalene on Easter morning 'with the warmth of his presence', or the disciples on Easter evening, 'inflaming their hearts in faith' on the road to Emmaus.[14]

This immediacy of the Son of God gets translated, when one starts talking about prayer, by the term 'indwelling'. The promise goes back to Paul ('Christ in you') and to the Johannine Jesus ('I in you').[15] He is so close as to be 'in' us. But 'in' dynamically, 'seeking' us, forming us to be, loving us into friendship. He is 'in', at our 'centre'; and, where 'one degree of love' unites us to God at our centre,[16] to meet God in prayer means to enter in, love and be loved there.

> 'Enter within your heart, and work in the presence of your Bridegroom, who is always present, loving you . . .'[17]

The gospel has eyes and they pierce to the soul. What John said about God's loving gaze has its place here. That gaze guarantees the possibility of prayer. It is the risen Christ, universally available.

Simon Peter in St Luke's account provides an image of such prayer. He met the eyes of Jesus in Galilee and dropped to his knees: 'Depart from me, for I am a sinful man, O Lord'. Jesus's gaze, confirming his words, changed him: 'Do not be afraid' (Luke 5:1–11). Their eyes met at the supper when the Master saw through his protestations of loyalty, but held out hope to him of 'turning' and becoming strong (22:32). At the time of failure too 'the Lord turned and looked at Peter'; the gaze undid Peter from the inside, and he went out and 'wept bitterly' (22:62). Their eyes met once more. The report is rather cryptic (what must it have been like?): 'The Lord has risen indeed, and has appeared to Simon!' (24:34).

'Risen indeed', and so alive in each person's history, gazing into each one's story, not just benignly, but effectively. As John's own history had taught him, 'For God, to gaze is to love and to work favours.' His love acts. It makes us 'worthy and capable of his love'. His gaze is his love and his love does things. 'God's gaze works four blessings in the soul: it cleanses her, makes her beautiful, enriches and enlightens her.'[18]

This meeting of eyes, hidden and spiritual, is what is taking place when we pray in faith and love.

The implications of John's statement are astounding: 'For God to love the soul means for him in some way to take her and place her in himself, making her like himself'.[19] When we pray, when we turn to God in friendship, believing his presence and desiring, loving him, then, for all its apparent bleakness, something is happening. God is taking us into himself and making us like himself. Those unspectacular periods of dry prayer conceal a whirlwind of activity, a current of relationship which cannot but transform us in its flow: '. . . making her like himself, and so he can love her in and with himself'.[20]

This is the mystic's testimony to the event of prayer in faith. It may well not describe what we feel. But it is encouraging to be told that this is the reality, though we cannot feel it.

Is prayer – not just words, or even a technique of silence, but prayer as an encounter with the living God – is prayer possible, now, for me? Here is John's contribution. Christ's loving gaze is constantly upon us, and *he* makes it possible.

# 20: Prayer, a 'Being With'

Given a sense of the vitality of prayer, as a supreme value, and a real possibility, then the practice of it becomes easier to handle. John's vision presents us, not with a blank page and the command, 'Fill it', but with something that is taking place, and with that invitation, 'Step into it, be part of it'.

The happening is God present within us, giving himself. That is John's exultant answer to his own tense question, 'Where?'

> 'Oh soul, most beautiful among all creatures, you who so long to know the place where your beloved is, so as to seek him and become one with him, now it has been stated: you yourself are the home in which he dwells . . . Here is a reason to be happy; here is a cause for joy: the realisation that every blessing and all you hope for is so close to you as to be within you.'

John grounds the answer in Scripture: 'The kingdom of God is within you' (Luke 17:21); 'You are God's temple' (2 Cor. 6:16). Then he draws from it an answer to our question, 'How?'

> 'Be glad, find joy there, gathered together and present to him who dwells within, since he is so close to you; *desire him there, adore him there*, and do not go off looking for him elsewhere . . . There is just one thing: even though he is within you, he is hidden.'[1]

That is John's description of the encounter of prayer, which opens us to the impact of God and helps change the world: 'Desire him there, adore him there.'

The description encapsulates John's message. It begins with a gift: a God who is 'close', who 'dwells within'. It invites us to make space for that gift – not 'going off' looking 'elsewhere'. It allows God to empty in us his own space, through the pain of his remaining 'hidden'. But here and now it means encounter, in faith and love ('adore', 'desire') an encounter which, at a deep level, changes us.

John's description – desire, adore, within – opens the way for a growing simplification of one's relationship with God. We shall come to this shortly. But already John has implied something very practical. Entry within means entry into Christ, 'the living image within'. To approach him guarantees the encounter. So John invites us to 'handle' his 'mysteries', to 'turn them over' in faith, that love might 'disclose what faith contains: the Bridegroom'.[2] He is encouraging us to meet Christ who is alive within us by focusing on him in his gospel life.

Christ's resurrection means that what he was then, he is for us now, and we can find him now as they found him then. We are being invited to think of him, talk with him, adore, desire, be anxious or sorry, be grateful and praise; to look at him, as he looks at us.

While John's writings can take this recourse to the gospel for granted,[3] in his live teaching he was eloquent on the point. There exists a report of his advice to his novices, new arrivals who wanted to know what to do during that hour in which they were supposed to be praying.[4] It is a simple, helpful method:

*'The first thing is to summon up the mysteries [of Jesus . . .] by imagining them.'*
Be present to Jesus as he sits wearied at the well, hot, alone, waiting (John 4). 'Imagine', not in detail, but impressionistically, as entering, not just observing.
*'Then ponder in your mind the mystery you have evoked.'*
Jesus is there, weary, for me . . . He demands no explanation; he wants to quench thirst with living water . . . He allows me to be with him.
*'Third, attentiveness to God, in loving stillness: this is where the fruit of the other activities is plucked, and where the door of the mind is opened to God's light . . .'*
Attentive in love; desire him there; adore him there; be with him in faith.

Again, 'summon up the mysteries': Jesus enters the room,

through the closed doors, stands among us, and breathes 'Peace' (John 20).

'Ponder the mystery': the risen Jesus has power to pass through barriers, our barriers, to speak the peace we need, to breathe his Spirit over the waters of chaos.

'Attentiveness in love', looking at him, opening to him as he looks at, speaks peace to, breathes on us.

The mysteries: Jesus, walking with the crowd, approached by the woman with the haemorrhage which the physicians could not cure; she touches him, power goes out from him; 'Who touched me?'; 'Your faith has made you well' (Mark 5).

Ponder: my, our, their, inner bleeding; Jesus's desire to heal; we touch him by believing; his power reaches in.

Attentive: reach out for his garment, and, taking the ache inside us, hold on to him in faith; allow his love and power to search out the haemorrhage within.

Once we are with the gospel Christ, the gaze of faith, the mutual presence in love, maintains a living contact. It puts us in place before the radiating gaze of the living God. We are asked to be awake there. We can rest there, till we find we need to strengthen the gospel framework again. In that contact God is building up his life in us, communicating himself to us; the touch of two vitalities which cannot but leave the inmost person changed.

It is that touch of vitalities which inspires John's description of prayer in *Canticle*: 'Desire him there, adore him there'. It implies a meeting of persons, and suggests a growth in prayer where those persons are allowed to be more themselves. John's God is an active God; so prayer is deeper where God acts more.[5] John views the person as an openness to God; so prayer will be more 'prayer' the more in touch with my need I am. He regards the two as bridegroom and bride; so prayer is most prayer when it simplifies into 'a work of love'.[6] We shall look at those possibilities for growth now.

## To be with God

As with the director, so with the person, 'the principal agent, and guide, and motive force in this matter is not them, but the Holy

Spirit, who never fails in his care . . .'7 The outpoured Spirit, fruit of the risen Christ, claims prayer as God's enterprise. That allows John to relax. It gives him great freedom and appreciation when he is faced by different styles of prayer that people may have. When Christ is as risen as that, *he* has to be the way of prayer, and any method is good so long as it engages with him.

The Our Father is good; praising is good; pleading is good; set or spontaneous, shared or alone, spoken or sung or silent, Scripture and psalms and liturgy and stillness, chapel or garden or mountain or car park – all this prayer is very good, if, by believing and loving, we are attending to the other Person.[8] John has, then, great appreciation. His intention is not to draw up a scale of excellence, and rivalry between methods and movements would for him be an irrelevance. When 'the Master is here and wants to see you', most differences are relativised.[9]

Having said that, if our need is for Christ, and Christ is present, gazing, giving himself, then prayer contains an impulse towards simplicity. Prayer can be a 'being with'.

John uses those terms; 'to be with' – an attentive presence to the other. The value of love was described in those terms: '. . . if they spent even half of this time *being with God* in prayer'.[10]

The same wording occurs when John reacts to the nearness of a concealed God: 'Well then, soul of beauty! Since you now know that in your heart your Beloved, for whom you long, dwells hidden, your concern must be to *be with him* in hiding, and there in your heart you will embrace him.'[11]

As for the living reality for which lesser joys must be surrendered: when people have found a location that helps them to pray, they should not merely get stuck on the scenery. Instead, 'forgetting the place, they should do their best to *be with God* within'.[12] This responds to the efforts of the Other, 'delighting to be with the sons of men', 'that is, when their delight is to *be with me*, who am the Son of God'.[13]

Beyond praise, petition, or begging for pardon, the impulse in prayer is towards presence, being with, being with the person. This must be so. Otherwise, we would be cheated of our Christian inheritance. The Son who elected to 'be with' us has opened new possibilities in prayer. In the gospels people do indeed ask Jesus for things, and praise him for his ministry. But there is a deeper movement, expressed by the attitude of the sinners whose concern is to 'sit with' him (Mark 2:15), whose happiness is to know themselves 'received' by him (Luke 15:2). The apostles' primary call is 'to be with him' (Mark 3:14). In John's gospel, this is the fruit of Jesus's resurrection: 'abide in my love' – remain, stay with, be with (John 15:9).

As this movement, from detail to presence, is an appropriate development in friendship (a point comes where we do not need to keep talking) so for John it is a normal development in prayer.[14] 'Desire him there, adore him there.' The images and words of Scripture, the requests and gratitude they inspire, the framework of thought and picture they create, these do not need to be constantly reinvented. They establish a communion which, once established, need not collapse if the scaffolding is removed. Should the communion weaken, then the detail is there to confirm it again.[15] But the communion is primary. If God is indeed giving himself, our task is to be in place to receive. The gaze of faith keeps us in that place. We are not told to keep extracting his love; we are told to abide in it.

## Simplicity and contemplation

We can abide in his love because his love abides. The resurrection, the gaze of the risen Christ, God's self-lavishing presence at the centre of the person, this ensures the possibility of contact, ensures that in 'being with him', something is taking place.

What John calls 'contemplation' is a special instance of this, a powerful impress of the resurrection on the world. It is special, not as esoteric, but as manifesting the reality of prayer with particular intensity. When he spoke about the bewilderment that goes with night, he was thinking particularly of the loss of the familiar at the onset of contemplative prayer.[16] But in itself, this night of prayer means positive growth. It is the gaze of Christ laying claim on the person at increasingly deep levels. It is a more total communication of God.

God, communicating himself, longs not to rest on the surface, but to feed and hold the *whole* person. John calls this inflow a 'dark, general loving knowledge'. Dark: deeper than thought and feeling. General: personal, total, free from refraction. This is presence – God imposing upon the other the demands of love which wants 'to be with'.

Here especially John encourages simplicity in one's response – the whole of me engaging a total gift:

'Then the soul too should go on just with a loving attentiveness to God, without making detailed acts, being open to what is happening in her . . . with a simple and open loving attentiveness, like someone opening their eyes with the attentiveness of love.'[17]

Opening their eyes with the attentiveness of love: John keeps coming back to this contemplative prayer, which marks a new phase of divine initiative. He does so, because the required simplicity may not come naturally. To a person used to waiting on the master at table, the invitation to sit down instead and eat with him will be confusing. The person may want to say, Have I done something wrong? Doesn't he *want* me to serve him? Perhaps I ought to improve my waiting skills?

Contemplation is faith spreading out. Faith had been a meeting hidden in the depths of the spirit. Now it is beginning to impress its hiddenness on the feelings and the mind. Now, not just my 'centre', but the circles of thought and sensitivity around the centre are being claimed by God. Though the real effect is that they now belong to him, the felt result is that they do not belong to me. His approach registers as darkness.

The person who used more or less to control her religious world with images, words and feelings, cannot but feel disconcerted when this activity of hers no longer seems to yield God. When God circumvents our radar, the instruments we once employed to connect with him are going to feel redundant, and his deeper presence will go unnoticed, until we adjust our expectations. The temptation is to keep fiddling with the control panel ('at least I'm doing something'). A better alternative, John suggests, is to surrender. Surrender, and be with the one who is content to be with us.

Not every darkness is contemplative, deriving from this 'excessive light'. Not all dryness in prayer is blessed. On the contrary, John can call dryness the 'cold north wind' which freezes the opening buds and hinders growth. When that wind blows, call on the south wind to warm the garden and spread perfume: 'Come south wind', the Holy Spirit, whose breeze communicates 'the Bridegroom, the Son of God'.[18]

Not every darkness is blessed; but every darkness can be turned to blessing. It may not be blessed, because it may result from a loss of interest in God: yes, I spend time in prayer, but it does not hold me; really my energy comes from somewhere or someone else. My efforts to pray then are distracted because love's moorings have come loose.

If so, this can be turned to blessing. I may now ask for the gift of forgiveness. I may begin again, with the inestimable advantage of knowing my inconsistency, and so shifting confidence from myself to God.

Alternatively, darkness may result from my state of mind or health: I have been unwell, work is difficult, these people are excluding me, I'm just feeling down . . . and, on top of all this, prayer feels impossible.

If so, this can be turned to blessing. I may now choose to be with God, choose it, even though I am receiving no feedback and my heart is like lead. John holds that this naked choice for God is most precious to God.[19] The perseverance works like sandpaper smoothing out a space which God will not fail to fill.

A third possibility: the darkness may be contemplative; it may result from the approach of God's excessive light, where I must surrender in loving attentiveness. If so, this can be turned to blessing – if I do not lose my nerve at the apparent emptiness.

Not every feeling of rootlessness is, then, to be welcomed. If it derives from apathy, surrender to it would be fatal; if it comes from being ill, sad, or off form, then going with that flow would make the depression worse. Because of this, John offers indications for when the inner bewilderment derives not from these but from contemplative light:

'The signs of inner recollection are three: first, the soul is not hankering after passing things; second, she has a love for solitude, silence and whatever will bring her to wholeness; third, the things that used to help – like series of reflections . . . – now get in the way, and she brings to prayer no other support than faith, and hope, and charity.'[20]

As John expresses these signs elsewhere, (1) I cannot pray as I used to. Perhaps mechanically I could say the prayers or think the pictures, but this would not be feeding me, it would not be real. (2) It is not that I am looking for an alternative to God. I am not coming to him with a divided heart. (3) In this emptiness, I have (initially) an anxiety to find him, or (once I have adjusted) a

contentment in being with him. This being alone, in love, attentive
to God, is home.[21]

These are indications of when it is right to surrender to the
darkness of prayer because it comes from God himself. The
second sign suggests that the darkness is not the result of apathy
or compromise; the third, that it is not just because I am off
form. I cannot pray as I used to; I do not want an alternative;
I do want God. Those are symptoms of a stillness that comes
from God. Here above all the advice applies: courage, patience,
without undue pain, trusting in God, in loving attentiveness.[22]

However, John's contribution goes further. Given the symptoms, we may need something more immediate than a diagnosis.
Suppose my 'darkness' is the result of my loss of interest; or
because I am overtired; or even if it is contemplative – the net
impression is that God is absent. That can paralyse any effort to
go forward at all. If I am turning again to prayer, here especially
I may be crippled by the feeling of being in the wrong place even
to start.

This is why John's witness to the way God is has practical
importance in prayer. 'If the soul is seeking God, much more is
her beloved seeking her.'[23] Wider than specific signs, he is holding
out the promise of an inflowing God. Wherever the darkness
comes from (lukewarmness, indisposition, contemplative growth),
John's witness confirms that now, for me, in my weakness, prayer
is possible: possible, because God never ceases to press in upon
my spirit; possible because Christ has not stopped welcoming the
weak; possible because I can decide now, again, to be with him,
to want to be with him.

### 'Within'

What of preparation, posture or gesture in prayer? John says little
about these. Not that they were unimportant to him: he prayed in
prison, crouching on the floor of his cell;[24] in Segovia, he prayed
at night beneath the trees, his arms outstretched, or looking out
to the Sierra Guadarrama from a small cave in the hillside.[25] But
in his writings the principal directive is that we should pray 'within'
– 'to be within with God'.[26]

Within: if prayer is the mutual presence of persons, then the preparation will be to find that point where I am most available as a person. To express this, John employs the language of 'recollection', the necessary response to an 'indwelling' God.

In sixteenth-century Spain, 'recollection' came to denote a technique of prayer, a concentration of one's psychological resources and entry into the inner world. It gave its name to a whole movement of spirituality. For John, concentration has more to do with the heart than with the brain. Our point of greatest openness on to God is our desire: 'What prepares the person to be united with God is the desire for God.'[27] Ordering one's loves, and acting out of love, is what 'gathers' the person for prayer.

Conversely, distraction means less the wandering of the imagination (can be unavoidable, says John);[28] more the dispersion which comes from desires that get out of hand. It involves not just my thoughts, but me. It has a magnetic force. The real distraction works by suction. My ego gets glued to it, and I'm off:

> I hold this person before you Lord; he is obviously suffering . . . Mind you . . . is it surprising? He is just so taken up in his own role. No one's going to trust him if he carries on like that . . . He never seems to notice me . . . He seems to think I make no contribution at all . . . Yesterday he definitely ignored me – just then when the others came in . . . as if it was all his work. Next time he asks for help I'll say it – 'I don't think you really need help from me' – and if he so much as . . .

When my sense of place is threatened, then times of prayer understandably mutate into an effort to defend my status. That is when I start composing and delivering speeches to this unacceptable person who really should know where he or she stands.

When this project, that relationship, is my centre of interest, then in times of prayer these understandably suck me on to themselves. This is when I fantasise my way through a story of success or romance.

In the face of distractions like these, to 'enter within', to become recollected, means resisting the pull to patch up my wounded ego or cheaply to satisfy my loneliness. It means owning my truth (this is how I am feeling), and affirming a love for the Christ who is seeking me even in that. Affirming, then, 'I want *you*; I want to want you.'

To quote one of John's more clinical expressions:

'When the soul gathers its joy, away from sensual things, it recovers from the dispersal into which it had fallen through its over-sensitised life, and is gathered together in God.'[29]

Reaching the point where I am most available as a person does involve an effort of mind: withdrawing from useless worry,[30] gathering in from compulsive dispersal, and, instead, homing in on this Person in this moment. It involves the intention, even if success is spasmodic. We are allowed to say, 'I can't focus'; but it is important to want and to try to focus.

Reaching that point involves, too, a physical alertness. So with posture, location: if lying down leads to sleep, not the best posture; if kneeling leads to backache, probably not either. Probably not in the park if I only get mesmerised by the passersby, nor with this or that music if it just sits in me as music. John affirms (perhaps autobiographically) that people can be greatly helped to 'find joy in God' by natural or artistic beauty.[31] But these must be held without glue on one's hands. Find the place, the posture, the sounds that help your spirit 'solidly and directly to rise to God'.[32]

So choose an appropriate place. If this is impossible, choose an inappropriate one. But choose one. If the freedom of the other Person is the decisive factor in prayer, then environment cannot be an ultimate problem – nor can 'the wrong conditions' be a real excuse.

Not every place is equally conducive for the mind; but any place can hold my desire. Being recollected involves unifying my life around the single desire, to please God: real 'devotion' 'consists in persevering there with patience and humility, distrusting oneself, only to *please God*'.[33]

This means learning not simply a technique, but a way of living – living for and with Another. Where this is my priority, difficulties in prayer turn out to be so many occasions on which I am affirming my option for God. Praying in the midst of a crammed timetable or a noisy household may not be especially satisfying; but it is a doubly powerful invitation to the One who is waiting for our desire: 'You show yourself first and you come out to meet those who desire you.'[34]

### 'Within' but 'hidden'

John has led us on a search for encounter with God. He has done so in the assurance of the resurrection – under the impact of a God who is pouring himself out. This God searches out the person, and makes them capable of the gift that will fill them. Something is happening, and, as John has been saying, it is a blessing to be part of it.

We have been told, too, that we may not *see* it happening. John's quest is for encounter, not for a feeling of encounter, for a God who communicates himself, but 'at least in a hidden way'. The godless bits of prayer may be the most apparent.

The description of prayer sounds serene: desire, adore, be with. This may indeed be one's experience. But it is possible that the would-be tranquillity of prayer is the very place in which my anxieties, scruples, guilt, anger, previously anaesthetised by the pace of life, now surface and make any contact with God feel impossible.

The natural reaction is to try mentally to sort out my anxieties, rearrange my disordered feelings, in short, tidy up my interior world before I risk any kind of encounter. While it is indeed necessary to ask God's forgiveness and want peace with my brother or sister, this other effort to 'set right' or 'work through' may be mistaken.

The most real thing about us, we heard John say, is our need for God. But this need is also our greatest claim. 'The immense love of Christ the Word cannot bear to see one who loves him suffer, without coming to her aid.'[35] If our anxieties are, at root, tokens of our deeper need, then when it begins to ache, when it cuts into our flesh, this is not an obstacle to prayer. It can be the point which opens on to God. Rather than first dressing the wound with analyses and excuses, John would have us locate the wound, and, without explanation, stand in it, hold it, before God.

Jesus' Mother is John's model here: when she perceived the couple's embarrassment at Cana, she did not propose a solution to her son. She simply held out to him the need. Not, 'You should do this'; but, 'They have no wine'.[36]

'They have no wine'; 'I have this difficulty'; 'this is the way I am feeling'. Our anxiety is itself language enough: to be with Christ, holding that before him, is communication. It provides its own way of prayer.

If my spirit is bleeding inside, I can approach him with that and grasp the hem of his garment. My prayer can be holding that garment; power continues to go out from him. If my spirit aches sorrow or loneliness, I can sit with him as at table, in a prayer that holds that ache before him; his presence still speaks welcome and healing into that. If I am aware of the waters of death, prayer can mean stretching out my hand, in the faith that he clasps my wrist. Prayer could be staying with that: the hand clasping the wrist.

John's story began here, with his need for the one who had 'wounded' him. There he found Christ, poor enough to share the wound, risen enough to heal it. Out of that, he confidently proposes prayer to us, not as an escape from the darkness that lies beyond our threshold, but as a journey into it. Prayer renames that darkness, not chaos, but the inner cavern, the space within the heart of the risen Christ.

\* \* \*      \* \* \*      \* \* \*

'You will not take from me, my God, what you once gave me, in your only Son Jesus Christ, in whom you gave me all I desire; so I shall rejoice: you will not delay, if I do not fail to hope . . .
    Mine are the heavens, and mine is the earth; mine are the peoples, the just are mine, and mine the sinners; the angels are mine, and the Mother of God, and all things are mine, and God himself is mine and for me, because Christ is mine and all for me.'[37]

As we come to the end of this sounding of John of the Cross, we find ourselves welcoming the universe. The impact of Christ upon him has flung open the horizons of his hope for the world. He has announced a God who, since the resurrection, is pressing in upon us; who, if we open to him, does indeed fill us in our life; and who, where we cannot open, himself works to cleave an opening. The immediacy of Christ is John's word of hope to people who feel incapable of change. And the encounter of prayer, the prayer of believing love, sets that change in motion.
    God's work of change John has called 'night'. Prayer leads us into that. It puts us in touch with our poverty. That is a safe place to be, because the Christ who gives is the one who has first shared, shared the night, searching out our poverty and 'being' there.

In saying that, John's word of hope flings open for us too the horizons of the world. Hearing of a Christ who is ours, the peoples become ours, the just and the sinful, and Christ invites us to serve them. Those who pray bear responsibility for the world.

In taking us into our poverty, prayer sets us at the centre point where the pain of our brothers and sisters converges. It sets us at the heart of the world's suffering. At night, colours disappear and new forms of perception come into play. In prayer, distance disappears and new veins of communication open up. The gospel has eyes which reach out and heal; and prayer can serve, by entering the pain of the brother and sister and holding it before the gaze of Christ.

We called John's Christ the understanding Christ, who 'knows what it is like to be me'. We can 'be with' him, because, in our degradation, he has first elected to be with us. As he is committed to us, so now he shares with us his commitment to all things; to the earth, the heavens, the sinners, and all peoples. Sounding John's soul, we have come to that threshold. This Christ is the all-embracing Christ: he invites us to be with him, that he, through us, may be with them.

# Notes

## Abbreviations

Works by John of the Cross:
*1A: Ascent of Mount Carmel* book one
*2A: Ascent of Mount Carmel* book two
*3A: Ascent of Mount Carmel* book three
*P*: prologue; *A P*: prologue to the *Ascent*, etc.
*1N: Night* book one
*2N: Night* book two
*CA: Canticle* (first redaction)
*CB: Canticle* (second redaction)
*LF: Living Flame* (second redaction)
*BMC* (*Biblioteca Mistica Carmelitana*, ed. P. Silverio, Burgos 1931) refers to the enquiry processes for beatification and canonisation (preparatory to John's being declared a saint) in which contemporary witnesses testified to John's character.

The works of John of the Cross referred to ('*Obras*') are those edited by José Vicente Rodríguez and Federico Ruiz, *Obras Completas*, Madrid, EDE 1993.
References to Crisógono de Jesús, *Vida de San Juan de la Cruz*, Madrid, BAC 1982 appear below as 'Crisógono'.
Other works, referred to by author and date:
Eulogio Pacho *San Juan de la Cruz y sus escritos* Madrid, Ediciones Cristiandad 1969;
Federico Ruiz: *Místico y Maestro* Madrid, EDE 1986, *Introducción a San Juan de la Cruz*, Madrid, BAC 1968, and 'Cimas de contemplación', *Ephemerides Carmeliticae* 13 (1962) 257–98.

Translations from Teresa de Jesús, Thérèse of Lisieux, Dámaso Alonso, and witnesses to John are mine unless specified otherwise. Emphasis in the texts is mine, except in the case of Thérèse of Lisieux.

## Chapter 2: Echoing the Impact

1. Testimony of Ana María, *BMC* 14.300.
2. Testimony of Francisca de San Eliseo, Crisógono 180 n. 27.
3. Letter 19, to Juana de Pedraza, 12/10/1589.
4. Testimony of Pablo de Santa María, Crisógono 412 n. 29; cf. pp. 412–13.
5. Testimony of Fray Lucas de San José, *BMC* 14.283.
6. Teresa de Jesús, *Way of Perfection* 1.5.
7. Teresa de Jesús, Letter 19, to her brother Lorenzo, 17/1/1570, translated by E. Allison Peers in *The Letters of Saint Teresa* Sheed and Ward, London 1980 vol. 1, p. 75.
8. Letter 13, to Francisco de Salcedo, September 1568 (from Teresa's *Obras Completas*, Madrid 1984). Forensic tests give John's height as 1.60 m. (5'3").
9. Teresa de Jésus *Foundations* 3.17.
10. Letter 268 to Ana de Jesús, November 1578.
11. Letter 13, to Francisco de Salcedo, September 1568.
12. José de Jesús María Qurioga, *Historia de la vida y virtudes del Venerable P. Fr. Juan de la Cruz* . . . Brussels 1628, I, 48, 194, resuming the testimonies of witnesses.
13. Letter 211, to King Philip II, 4/12/1577.
14. Testimonies of Ana de San Bartolomé (in her *Obras Completas* I, 65); Ana de San Alberto (BMC 10.401); and of Inocencio de San Andrés, *BMC* 14.66
15. Testimony of Inocencio de San Andrés, Crisógono 156 n. 49.
16. Testimony of the nuns of Sabiote, in Pacho p. 111.
17. Testimony of Alonso de la Madre de Dios, *BMC* 14.387.
18. Letter 250, to Jerónimo Gracián, 19/8/1578.
19. See Letter 1, to Catalina de Jesús, 6/8/1581.
20. *2N* 6.1, see Mt 12:40.
21. *CB P* 1; see *P* 2.
22. *CB P* 1.
23. *CB* 13.
24. *2N* 11.7.

## Chapter 3: Picking Up the Echo

1. Letter 268 to Ana de Jesús, November 1578.
2. Alonso de la Madre de Dios relates this (see José Vicente Rodriguez, '¿San Juan de la Cruz, talante dialogal?', *Revista de Espiritualidad* 1976 pp. 512–13).
3. *BMC* 13.389, 391.
4. Quiroga *Historia* III, 3, 380.
5. See Francisca's letter to Jerónimo de San José, 9/11/1629, and *BMC* 14.170.
6. *LF* 3.59.
7. *1A* 9.1.

8. *CB* 23.6.
9. *2A* 17.3.
10. *CB P* 2.
11. *CB* 34.4.
12. *2A* 5.7 and 26.6.
13. Testimony of Magdalena del Espíritu Santo, *BMC* 10.325.
14. *A P* 3.
15. *1A* 8.4, see *A P* 6 & 8.
16. *A*, Outline ('*argumento*').
17. *CB* 39.4; 38.3; 35.1; 29.3.
18. *LF* 3.27.
19. *CB* 39.7, see *2A* 7.12.
20. *CB* 1.1.

## Chapter 4: A Quiet Man Speaks

1. Testimony of a nun in BMC 10.131; cited in John of the Cross *Obras* p. 92.
2. See *LF* 1.15; 3.1.
3. Letter 5, June 1586 to Ana de San Alberto. Details of John's travelling are provided by Girolamo Salvatico in *Dios Habla en la Noche* (Various authors, Madrid, EDE 1990) p. 303.
4. *BMC* 10.31.
5. Letter 31, to Ana de Peñalosa, 21/9/1591.
6. Ibid.
7. *LF* (first redaction) *P* 4.
8. *LF* (first redaction) *P* 1.
9. *LF* (first redaction) *P* 3.
10. *LF* 2.10; 3.68; 2.8; see Ruiz (1986) p. 284.
11. *LF* 2.21.
12. *LF* (first redaction) 4.17.
13. Dámaso Alonso 'La poesía de San Juan de la Cruz (desde esta ladera)', *Obras Completas* vol. 2, Madrid 1973, p. 1015.
14. See Mk 2:19; Jn 3:29; Eph. 5:22–32; Rev. 21:9.
15. *LF* 1.2; see 2.15.
16. So Ruiz (1962) p. 268.
17. *LF* 1.8.
18. *LF* 2.2.
19. *LF* 1.9; 2.36.
20. *LF* 3.79.
21. *LF* 1.5, 7, 4.
22. *LF* 2.16; 1.3, 6.
23. *LF* 2.36.
24. *LF* 1.8.
25. *LF* 3.6.
26. Ibid.
27. *LF* (first redaction) 2.6.
28. *LF* 2.3; see CB 28.1.

158 *The Impact of God*

29. *LF* 1.28, 23.
30. *LF* 1.9; 3.10.
31. *LF* 3.18, 22.
32. *LF* 2.22.
33. *LF* 2.34; Gal. 2:20.
34. *LF* 1.1.
35. *LF* 1.17.


## Chapter 5: The Gospel Has Eyes

1. *CA* 11.4.
2. See Henri de Lubac, *Catholicism: a study of the corporate destiny of mankind*, Burns and Oates 1950, p. 181.
3. *CB* 19.6.
4. *CB* 33.1.
5. *CB* 32.5.
6. Ibid.
7. Letter 13, to a Carmelite friar, (?) 14/4/1589.
8. *LF* P 1; 3.80.
9. *LF* 4.7.
10. *Sayings* 99.
11. *Canticle*, stanza five.
12. *CB* 5.4; Gen. 1:31.
13. *CB* 5.4.
14. *CB* 6.1.
15. *LF* 3.27.
16. See *LF* 3.28–67.
17. *LF* 3.27–8.
18. *LF* (first redaction) P 1.
19. Letter 28, to Ana de Peñalosa, 19/8/1591.
20. *CB* 1.4.
21. Letter 23, to a directee (uncertain date).
22. *LF* 3.26.
23. *2A* 4.6.
24. *LF* P 2.
25. *LF* 2.5; 2.21; 2.36.
26. *LF* 1.15, alluding to Js 1:17, Isa. 59:1, Eph. 6:9, Wisd. 6:16.
27. *Sayings* 2.
28. *LF* 4.9.


## Chapter 6: The Right Kind of Emptiness

1. Hans Urs von Balthasar (quoting H. Delacroix), in *The Glory of the Lord* (Edinburgh, T. & T. Clark 1986), vol. 3, p. 133 n. 124.
2. *LF* 3.28.
3. *LF* 2.27; see *1A* 5.2.

4. *1A* 13.11; sketch and notes in John of the Cross *Obras* pp. 133–6.
5. *LF* 1.3.
6. *LF P* 3; 1.3–4, 23, 33.
7. *LF* 1.19.
8. *LF* 1.15.
9. Letter 7, 18/11/1586.
10. *LF* 1.32.

## Chapter 7: Blockages

1. *2A* 14.14.
2. Testimony of Baltasar de Jesús (in Pacho (1969) p. 222).
3. *A P* 8; see *2A* 1.3.
4. *A P* 3, 8.
5. *1N* 6.2.
6. Letter 19, to Juana de Pedraza, 12/10/1589.
7. Quiroga, *Historia* I,1,369 (in Crisógono p. 281).
8. *1A* 3.4.
9. *1A* 9.2.
10. *3A* 15.1; *CB* 3.5.
11. *1A* 11.6.
12. *1A* 5.4.
13. *1A* 4.6.
14. *1A* 6.5.
15. *3A* 19.10.
16. *3A* 20.2.
17. *3A* 35.6; 38.1,5.
18. *1A* 4.8.
19. *1A* 11.4.
20. *1A* 11.2.
21. *Sayings* 140, 146–7.
22. Letter 3, to Ana de San Alberto, 1582.
23. *Sayings* 145, 152; Letter 19, to Juana de Pedraza, 12/10/1589.
24. *1A* 10.4; *3A* 25.4.
25. *Sayings* 15.
26. *1A* 13.11.

## Chapter 8: Some Kind of Remedy

1. *1A* 13.1.
2. *1A* 13.5–6.
3. *1A* 13.7,4; see Precautions 6; also Letter 21, to María de Jesús, 20/6/1590, (and note 2 there on 'endeavour').
4. *1A* 13.7.
5. *1A* 13.3–4.
6. *1A* 13.7.
7. *3A* 28.8; 30.5; 35.7; *2N* 19.4.

8. *Confessions* VIII v, xi, ix (translated F.J. Sheed, published Sheed and Ward 1951, pp. 129, 139, 137).
9. *1A* 1.4.
10. *1A* 14.2.
11. *1A* 13.3.
12. *LF* 1.8.
13. *CB* 31.2.
14. 'Prayer of a soul in love', *Sayings* 26.


# Chapter 9: 'Night'

1. *1A* 1.1. The original speaks here of '*noches*', plural.
2. *Night* introduction.
3. *1N* 13.3; see 8.2.
4. *2N* 7.3; see 7.4; 1.1; 14.3.
5. *2N* 6.1.
6. Roman Liturgy, *Rite of Holy Week*, Easter Vigil. John Sullivan OCD develops this, 'Night and light: the poet John of the Cross and the 'Exsultet' of the Easter Liturgy' (*Ephemerides Carmeliticae* 30 (1979) 52–68).
7. Testimony of Francisca de la Madre de Dios, *BMC* 14.169; cf. Crisógono p. 181.
8. *1N* 10.6; see 5.1.
9. Roman Liturgy, *Rite of Holy Week*, Easter Vigil.


# Chapter 10: There is Somewhere to go

1. *2N* 3.1.
2. *Canticle* B stanza 14.
3. Cristóbal Colón, [Christopher Columbus] *Los cuatro viajes* (ed. Consuelo Varela, Madrid 1986), entry for October 5th etc., first journey.
4. *LF P* 3.
5. *2N* 16.8.
6. *2A* 4.5; see *2N* 10.6.
7. *CB* 25.9–11.
8. *1A* 13.11.
9. *Sayings* 5–9.
10. *LF* 3.46.
11. This relation to Scripture and Church appears in the prologues to John's works. See also, *inter alia* *2A* 17.2; 19.9; 22.2; *CB* 7.6; and *2A* 22.11; 24.3; 27.4; *3A* 44.3 respectively.
12. *LF* 3.46.
13. *1N* 8.3.
14. See *1N* 12.3.
15. See *1N* 12.2–8; cf. *3A* 28.2; *1N* 2.1.
16. *1N* 12.3.

17. *1A* 10.4.
18. *1N* 13.7.
19. *1N* 4.8.
20. *2N* 11.4.
21. *2N* 11.7.
22. Testimony of Juan de Santa Ana, ms. 8568 fol. 404 (see John of the Cross, *Obras* pp. 1115f.).
23. Testimony of Catalina de San Alberto (Crisógono p. 403); see *BMC* 14.399.
24. *LF* 1.30.
25. *CB* 37.1.
26. *LF* 1.27.
27. *LF* 3.10; see 1.28, 'bringing her into that glory'; *CB* 26.2: 'gathering her into the inner spaces of his love'; *CB* 14.1; 22.6.
28. *LF* 3.10.

## Chapter 11: It Has to be God

1. *1A* 4–12.
2. *3A* 2.15; see *1A* 1.2; 13.1; *2A* 2.3; 6.8.
3. *1N* 1–7.
4. *1N* 7.1.
5. *3A* 9.2.
6. *1N* 5.1.
7. Ibid.
8. *1N* 5.3.
9. 1 Sam. 17:47; Ps. 113(112):7; *1N* 12.3.
10. *1N* 3.3.
11. 'Discovering Francis Thompson', Gregory Allen, *Mount Carmel* 49,2 (1992) pp. 81–92.
12. Denzinger–Schönmetzer 806 (see *The Teaching of the Catholic Church* ed. Karl Rahner, New York, Alba House 1971, p. 99).
13. *CB* 26.4.
14. *CB* 37.4.
15. *CB* 7.9.
16. *CB* 14.8.
17. *1N* 5.3.

## Chapter 12: Healing Darkness (I)

1. The 'Rule of the Order of the Blessed Virgin Mary of Mount Carmel', given by Albert, Patriarch of Jerusalem (AD 1206–14).
2. Letter of Marina de San Angelo, ms. 8568, 458–63 (printed in John of the Cross, *Obras* pp. 1126–7).
3. Testimony of Bernardo de la Virgen (Crisógono p. 396).
4. Letter 33, to a Carmelite nun, late 1591.
5. *LF* 3, 46–7, see Ps. 121 (120): 4.

## Chapter 13: Healing Darkness (II)

1. Testimony of Gabriel de la Madre de Dios (see Crisógono, p. 266).
2. Testimony of Martín de San José, *BMC* 13.378.
3. Testimony of Eliseo de los Mártires, *Dictámenes* 15 (printed in John of the Cross, *Obras* p. 1125).
4. Letter 26, to María de la Encarnación, 6/7/1591.
5. See *2A* 22.11, 13; *3A* 31.9; *Sayings* 43–5.
6. *LF* 2.30.
7. *Sayings* 4.
8. Testimonies of Jerónimo de la Cruz and of Beatriz de Jesús, in Crisógono p. 290.
9. This appears in *Dios Habla en la noche* (Various authors, Madrid, EDE 1990) p. 12.
10. *IN* 1.2; 8.3 [the object in the original is plural]; 12.1.
11. *LF* 3.66; see *A P* 3.
12. *2N* 5–7; *LF* 1.22–3.
13. See Letters 21; 15; 19; 22; 20; *Precautions* 15; *Counsels* 3–4.
14. *IN* 9.3.
15. *LB* 2.27.
16. *Master in Faith* (Apostolic Letter for the fourth centenary of the death of St John of the Cross) §14. (English translation, *L'Osservatore Romano* 24/12/1990). On what follows, see Ruiz (1968) pp. 525f.
17. *LF* 1.12.
18. *IN* 14.1–3.
19. *2N* 6.6.
20. *2N* 13.5; see *LF* 1.20.
21. *2N* 6.2,6.
22. Thérèse of Lisieux, *Manuscrits Autobiographiques*, translated by Ronald Knox as *Autobiography of a Saint* (Collins Fontana 1958, 1960) pp. 200–1.
23. *2N* 7.3.
24. *2N* 8.1; cf. Lamentations 3.29.

## Chapter 14: Beyond Sympathy

1. See *IN* 6.8.
2. *1A* 5.7.
3. *2A* 13; *IN* 9.
4. *2N* 19–20.
5. *Sayings* 26.
6. *IN* 10.3–4.
7. *3A* 41.2, 1.
8. *A P* 3.
9. Letter 28, to Ana de Peñalosa, 19/8/1591.
10. *IN* 9.8.

11. 'Manuscrit C' in *Oeuvres Complètes*, Cerf, Desclée de Brouwer 1992, p. 244: 'je chante ce que *je veux croire*'.
12. Letter of Juan Evangelista to Jerónimo de San José, 2/7/1630, quoted in John of the Cross *Obras* p. 1114.
13. Letter 19, to Juana de Pedraza, 12/10/1589.
14. Letter 15, 8/7/1589.

## Chapter 15: The Experience of God (I)

1. 1 Jn 4:4; see Rom. 8:35; Lk 12:32.
2. *2A* 24.8.
3. *3A* 27.5.
4. *3A* 30.5.
5. *LF* 3.46.
6. *2A* 29.4.
7. Karl Rahner *Meditations on Priestly Life*, London, Sheed and Ward 1973, p. 13. On the two sides of reality see his 'The eternal significance of the humanity of Jesus for our relationship with God', *Theological Investigations* vol. 3, London, Darton Longman and Todd 1967) pp. 35–6.
8. *CB* 38.8.
9. *CB* 26.4.
10. Luis de Góngora, *Sonetos Completos*, Clásicos Castilia, Madrid 1969, p. 149.
11. *LF* 2.10.
12. *1A* 9.1.
13. *Sayings* 34.
14. *LF* 3.22.
15. *CB* 1.12; see 1.4.
16. *CB* 1.11.
17. *2A* 9.1.
18. *3A* 7.2.
19. *3A* 30.4; see Letter 13, to a Carmelite friar, 14/4/1589 (?).
20. *CB* 11.11; see Ruiz (1968) pp. 443–74.
21. *3A* 8.5.
22. *2A* 27.4.
23. Letter 19, to Juana de Pedraza, 12/10/1589.
24. Letter 20, to a Carmelite nun, at Pentecost.
25. *BMC* 14.370.
26. *3A* 10.2.
27. *2A* 5.7.
28. *2A* 7.8.
29. See *2A* 11.
30. *2A* 29.5.
31. *2A* 8.4.
32. Cf. *3A* 2.1.
33. *2N* 21.11.
34. *LF* 2.27.

35. *2A* 5.7.
36. Council of Trent, session VI, decree on justification.
37. *LF* 3.80.
38. See *2A* 1.1; 24.4; *3A* 14.2.


## Chapter 16: The Experience of God (II)

1. *2A* 29.6; see 3.5.
2. *2A* 3.1.
3. *2A* 3.5.
4. *2A* 3.1; see 9.1.
5. *2A* 9.3; see 1.1; 9.2; *1A* 2.3–4; *2N* 2.5.
6. *2A* 9.3.
7. *CB* 12.1, 3; Jn 4:14; 7:39.
8. *CB* 12.4.
9. Cf. *3A* 1.1; *2A* 24.8; 29.6.
10. *CB* 2.6; 11.10; 39.10.
11. So Ruiz (1986) pp. 185–8. On the whole theme, André Bord *Mémoire et Espérance chez Jean de la Croix*, Paris 1971.
12. *3A* 5.2.
13. See *3A* 5.2; 6.3.
14. See *3A* 42.3.
15. *3A* 6.3.
16. Testimony of Martín de la Asunción, *BMC* 14.83–4.
17. *3A* 15.1.
18. *3A* 2.10.
19. Poem X, 'Tras de un amoroso lance', vv. 31–2; *3A* 7.2; *2N* 21.8; and testimony of Alonso de la Madre de Dios, *BMC* 14.371.
20. Letter 22, June 1590.
21. *3A* 3.6.
22. See *2A* 14.14; 11.13.
23. *LF* 2.7.
24. *LF* 2.10.
25. *CB* 11.11.
26. See *Sayings* 114; *2A* 5.7; *CB* 1.14; 26.14; 36.4.
27. *LF* 1.33; 1.8; 2.4; 3.1; *CB* 9.7.
28. *CB* 32.1 and 31.2; see *3A* 44.3.
29. *CA* 37.3.
30. Letter 33, to a Carmelite nun, late 1591.
31. Letter 13, to a Carmelite friar, (?) 14/4/1589.
32. *LB* 1.13.
33. See *1A* 4.3; 5.5.
34. *Sayings* 106.
35. See *2N* 13.9; *CB* 12.7–8; 28.1; 32.6; Letter 11, to Juana de Pedraza, 28/1/1589.
36. *CB* 19.6; 33.1; 32.6.
37. *LB* 3.46.
38. *CB* 33.8.

39. *CB* 29.2–3; see *LF* 1.3.

## Chapter 17: A Question About Jesus

1. Robert Bolt *A Man for All Seasons*, published by London, Heinemann 1960, pp. 85–6.
2. *2N* 6.2; 7.7; see 10.2; 13.5.
3. Karl Rahner, 'The eternal significance of the humanity of Jesus for our relationship with God', in *Theological Investigations* vol. 3, (London, Darton Longman and Todd, 1967) p. 42.
4. See Robina Rafferty, 'Open Doors – the Crisis of Homelessness', *Signum* 18/8 (1990) 58–61, p. 61; on what follows cf. Ruiz (1968) p. 361.
5. *2A* 7.12.
6. *BMC* 14.121.
7. Testimony of Isabel de la Encarnación, see Crisógono p. 192.
8. Letter 4, 1582.
9. *CB* 40.7.
10. *LF* 2.34; Gal. 2:20.
11. *1A* 13.4.
12. *2A* 15.4.
13. *2N* 13.6–7.
14. See e.g. *2A* 4.8; *3A* 17.2.
15. Teresa de Jesús *Foundations* 13.5. On the Ballads, see José Fradejas, 'Los Romances de San Juan de la Cruz', in *Simposio sobre San Juan de la Cruz*, ed. José Muñoz Luengo, Avila 1986, pp. 51–68.
16. *2N* 7.7.
17. 'Ballads' (B) vv. 57–8, 21, 32, 23.
18. B 45–6, see 13–16.
19. B 17–20.
20. B 77–8.
21. B 87.
22. B 99.
23. B 155–6, 165–6.
24. B 135–44, see 149–53.
25. *Summa Theologiae* III 1, 3.
26. Is 64:1 (63.19) (*Jerusalem Bible* translation, London, Darton Longman and Todd 1974); see B 185.
27. B 176–7, 180, 200.
28. B 229; see 229–44.
29. B 245–58.
30. B 259–66.

## Chapter 18: Jesus, the Experience Of God

1. *2A* 22.1.
2. *2A* 22.3.
3. Cf. *2A* 8.4.

4. *LF* 1.32.
5. *2A* 22.4; cf. *CB* 6.7.
6. *2A* 22.7, 11; 27.4; *3A* 42.6; 44.3.
7. *Sayings* 26.
8. *2A* 22.5.
9. *CB* 1.11 and title.
10. *CB* 6.7.
11. *CB* 37.3.
12. *CB* 37.5. On what follows see Karl Rahner, *Watch and Pray With Me*, Burns & Oates, 1968, pp. 17–18.
13. *CB* 14.8.
14. *CB* 37.4; see *CB P* 1; *2N* 20.4.
15. See *2A* 12.3.
16. *CB* 37.6.
17. *2A* 22.6.
18. *A P* 3–5; 1A 1.2; 13.1.
19. *2N* 22.2; see *3A* 2.15.
20. Cf. *2A* 7.1.
21. Mt. 7:14; Mk 8:34; Jn 12:25; Mt. 20:20–2, 11:30; Jn 10:9; in *2A* 7.2–8.
22. *2A* 7.5.
23. *2A* 7.9.
24. *2N* 6.2; 7.7.
25. *2A* 7.8–11; see Mk 15:34.
26. *LF* 2.21.
27. See Thomas Aquinas *Summa Theologiae* I 79.9 ad 3; III 46.7; 15.5 ad 3.
28. *LF* 2.2.
29. *CB* 29.2.
30. *2A* 7.11.
31. *IN* 1§1; *2N* 21.3.
32. *2N* 24.3.
33. *2N* 19.4; 13.6. On this theme see Lucien Marie, *L'Expérience de Dieu: Acualité du message de Saint Jean de la Croix*, Paris, 1968, p. 253 et al.
34. *IN* 6.7; 7.4; see *LF* 2.28, 'cross', 'gall' and 'vinegar'.
35. *2N* 6.5.
36. *2N* 6.1–2; see Letter 7 to the nuns in Beas, 18/11/1586.

## Chapter 19: Prayer: Should we? Can we?

1. Eliseus de los Mártires, 'Dictámenes', 15–19 (printed in John of the Cross, *Obras* p. 1125).
2. *2A* 21.5; see 2 Chr. 20:3–12.
3. *2A* 17.8.
4. 'Ballads' 77, see 111–24.
5. *CB* 23.3.
6. *CB* 29.2.

7. *2A* 7.11.
8. *CB* 29.3.
9. See *2A* 22.6,5.
10. *A P* 6.
11. Testimony of Elvira de San Angelo, interpreted by Crisógono pp. 351–2.
12. *3A* 35.5.
13. *3A* 40.1.
14. *3A* 31.8.
15. Col. 1:27 (see Rom. 8:10); Jn 15:4 (see 17:26).
16. *LF* 1.13; see 3.28.
17. *Sayings* 89.
18. *CB* 19.6; 32.6; 33.1.
19. *CB* 32.6.
20. Ibid.


# Chapter 20: Prayer, a 'Being With'

1. *CB* 1.7–8.
2. *CB* 1.11.
3. Cf. 2A 12.3.
4. José de Jesús María Quiroga, *Don que tuvo San Juan de la Cruz*, printed in Ruiz (1968) pp. 511–12.
5. *2N* 23.11.
6. *CB* 28.9.
7. *LF* 3.46.
8. See *3A* 44.4; 40.2; 42.6; 24.4; *CB* 25.4.
9. Jn 11:28 (*Jerusalem Bible* London, DLT 1974).
10. *CB* 29.3.
11. *CB* 1.10.
12. *3A* 42.2.
13. *CB* 17.10, and Prov. 8:31 (*Jerusalem Bible* London, DLT 1974).
14. See *2A* 14.2.
15. See *2A* 15.1.
16. See *2A* 12; *1N* 8.
17. *LF* 3.33; see *2A* 15.2.
18. *CB* 17.8.
19. *Sayings* 14, 19, 20.
20. *Sayings* 118; see *LF* 3.34.
21. *2A* 13; *1N* 9.
22. *1N* 10.3–4.
23. *LF* 3.28.
24. So Martín de la Asunción, *BMC* 14.96.
25. Testimonies of Elvira de San Angelo (Crisógono p. 337); and of Fray Bernabé de Jesús, *BMC* 14.294.
26. *3A* 42.2.
27. *LF* 3.26.
28. *2A* 13.3; 14.5.

29. *3A* 26.2.
30. *3A* 5.2–3.
31. *3A* 24.4.
32. *3A* 39.2.
33. *1N* 6.6.
34. *Sayings* 2.
35. *2N* 19.4.
36. Jn 2:3; *CB* 2.8.
37. 'Prayer of a soul in love', *Sayings* 26.

# Index